Elephants
I'll Never Forget

A Keeper's Life
at Whipsnade and London Zoo

John Weatherhead

The
Book
Castle

DEDICATION

I would like to dedicate this book to all those fortunate people everywhere who work with elephants.

****

First published July 2002 by
The Book Castle
12 Church Street
Dunstable
Bedfordshire LU5 4RU

ISBN 1 903747 16 3

Typeset & Designed by Priory Graphics, Flitwick, Bedfordshire.
Printed by Impress Print, Corby, Northants.

Front cover: John, with Katie, 1989. (CT)
Back cover: John, Sally and Carla training young elephants. (CT)

CONTENTS

About the Author

John Weatherhead was born in St. John's Wood, London in 1942. He was the fourth of a family of five. From the early age of six he knew he wanted to devote his life to animals.

After much persistence this was achieved by being offered a job as a helper at London Zoo at the age of 15. So began his 40 years association with a wide variety of wildlife in England and from throughout the world. But his special love and expertise became 'elephants' - hence this book.

Photographic References

AP	Associated Press Ltd
BH	Brian Harma
CM	Colin Mew
CT	Carla Tams
DD	Deputy Director, Kobe Oji Zoo, Japan
DT	The Daily Telegraph
E&P	Echo & Post Ltd
FP	Fox Photos Ltd
Fr	A Friend
EVB	Elli van den Brink
FVB	Frans van den Brink
JF	John Foster
JN	Japanese Newspaper
KC	Ken Crouch
LZ	Zoological Society of London
PA	Paul Anscombe
RS	Richard Sindry
TB	Tom Begg
SW	Sheila Weatherhead

Foreword by David Jones
formerly Director of Zoos, London and Whipsnade

"No job is more challenging, exciting or variable than that of the zookeeper. No day begins or ends in the same way, especially when your charges are as different as bears, birds of prey and especially elephants.

John Weatherhead started his working life with animals at a time when the Zoo in London was beginning to emerge from being just a 19th century menagerie to a fully fledged leader in an international animal conservation arena. John was able to take advantage of that period in the late 70's and 80's when the demand for the Society's services as consultant was beginning to grow.

He was a willing and able volunteer as we began helping zoos in the Middle East to establish their own national facilities. But zoos are also complex organisations, never large, but home to many specialised teams with many different skills. Not easily understood in that complexity by most, although most seem to 'know' how to run them!

This complexity creates some interesting management issues. London and Whipsnade were never recipients of the public resources they so richly deserved, so the Society faced a host of questions and problems in the late 80's and 90's, which resulted in it having to 'downsize' and become in many ways, more introspective. It lost its leadership and sense of initiative and John reflects that in the sad description of his own departure from his much loved Whipsnade.

Thankfully, after a decade in 'no man's land', there are signs of the organisation beginning to understand its true potential again. But it is thanks to people like John who helped bring it through a difficult but interesting period that it is able to do that today.

His diary of a thirty year relationship with this most fascinating but eccentric of organisations brought back to life many of the chapters in my own parallel life with the 'Society'. For anyone with an interest either in zoos or zookeeping in general or these two great zoos in particular, this is a very engaging story."

Tower of Ivory

Colin Mew, whose poem appears on the next pages, was a colleague and friend of mine for over 20 years. The poem was given to me as a gift and it seems a poignant, yet fitting and beautiful start to my book.

TOWER OF IVORY

They built an ivory tower
With every poacher's seere,
A monument to man's desire
To profit from the peer.

It covered many countries
And many paid to see
This pinnacle of fashion,
Born of fantasy.

Ivory stalls and tables
Stood along each wall
And every ivory ornament
Was sold upon them all.

It took a rich man's feelings
The building site to clear
And we have bought the poison
From every profiteer.

Beneath the tower's shadow
Where children never play
There is a walled enclosure
Where the air is still all day.

The grass is green all year because
Deep beneath the turf
Lies buried every elephant
That ever walked the earth.

Sometimes, when it's quiet
And you sit there all alone
The ground will start to tremble
And you'll hear a gentle moan.

And if it should be raining
So all the grass is wet
You will see each ivory blade,
Slowly bleed to death.

It makes no place for sleeping
That turns in every dream
A starving baby elephant
Wakes you with its scream.

The caring mother's gentleness
Resting in the sun:
A pile of rotting carcasses
Captured by the gun.

The wall was built on purpose
To keep this from your sight,
But that won't hide the emptiness
Which walks the plains at night.

A single grave has bred a pit
Grown deeper every year,
While each new sunrise finds the tower
Has grown another tier.

They built an ivory tower
Destined for the sky,
But the sun has caught its shallowness
And irritates the eye.

Then you turn your face away
And let your eyelids dry,
But you'll meet tomorrow's reason
As it goes marching by.

It takes greedy men and money
And you to pay the price,
But count the shadow's measure
And cost the sacrifice.

Colin Mew
December 1983

Acknowledgements

With special thanks for their assistance in helping to prepare this book to Margaret Bevan, Philip Bevan, Karen Baker and Sheila Weatherhead.

Carla Tams and the author - training young elephants.

CHAPTER 1
"The Beginning"

Like many small boys I always wanted to work with animals. I kept a variety of pets in the home in which I lived with my parents in St. John's Wood. Having tried the common household pets, I then ventured into lizards, slowworms and snakes. I used to visit my local pet shop to seek information regarding the correct way in which to look after and care for these animals.

On one occasion, I bought a corgi pup in Camden Town, which I kept under my bed for two days before my father was aware of its presence! Having discovered the pup, my father commented on the fact that the dog looked lethargic and suggested that we should pay a visit to the local veterinary surgeon who discovered that the pup was suffering from the first stages of distemper. He advised me to return it to the pet shop from whence it had come. After a lengthy discussion with my father, my £4.00 was returned forthwith, by a very disgruntled manager!

Another pet shop acquisition was Hammy, the hamster. He lived on the veranda of our third floor flat, in a sturdy cage made by my father. One of the house rules was that I kept all my pets outside because my mother was petrified of anything that moved fast along the ground.

One morning, on cleaning out the cage, Hammy decided to take a nose-dive to the lawn at ground level. I shot downstairs to retrieve my hamster before he escaped forever. With the animal on my shoulder I arrived at the front door and called to my mother through the letterbox. On approaching the front door she screamed and said, "You little sod!" I was unaware of the fact that Hammy had run down my arm, through the letterbox and fallen onto the floor inside beside my mother's feet! She ran out onto the veranda, screaming, locking the door behind her, with me outside. I climbed up the three verandas to reach my mother who gave me a clout both for climbing and also for letting the hamster loose on her.

Another pet was a ferret obtained through a friend of mine, which I kept in my modified hamster cage. This venture was short-lived due to the fact that it not only bit me frequently but also gave off a strong smell about which the neighbours below complained bitterly and threatened to inform the Council. So my old man paid yet another visit to the pet shop!

As a young lad it was very common for me to see many stray dogs loose on the London streets. Occasionally these dogs were rounded up by the Police and taken to St. Johnís Wood Police Station awaiting The Battersea Dogs Home van which came to transport them away on Friday mornings to the home.

Due to my love of animals, the thought of them being destroyed appalled me, so I went with my friend Kenny Brown to the rear of the station, on the night before, to release the dogs from the holding area. To achieve this we had to divert the attention of the police by creating a noise outside the front of the station. Whilst this was happening, I went around to the back and released the dogs for another week of freedom.

One of my favourite pastimes was to knock on peopleís doors and ask if I could take their dog for a walk. One of these was a Cocker Spaniel Cross Springer by the name of Bob. This dog had a skin problem, which the owners had discovered from the veterinary surgeon to be mange. His suggestion to them was that the dog should be destroyed. I begged with them to let me have the dog, and after numerous discussions they acceded to this idea. On my arrival home with the dog, my father suggested that I took him to the vet to be destroyed! I did take the dog to the vet for his advice and he said that there was a cure but it would be a painstaking job involving bathing the dog twice a day, in a sulphur solution, for six months. I achieved this and cured Bobby. Sadly, while Bobby was out with father, he ran under a double decker London bus and was killed outright. My father compensated me for this by giving me sixpence.

One of my other pastimes was to visit Regents Park and walk over to where I could see the monkeys on Monkey Hill in the zoo. One day Kenny Brown and I discovered we could push our heads through the bars and thereby achieve entrance to the zoo. This just enhanced my feeling that here was where I wanted to be.

On one of these unlawful visits to the zoo we were apprehended by a large uniformed man. We said that we were paying a visit with our

The old Parrot House from the South Gate of Regent's Park Zoo. (PA)

parents. He asked, "Are they members then?" I replied "Yes", to which he asked "Are they ordinary members, Fellows of the Society or Honorary Members of the Society?" He obviously deduced that we were lying and escorted us out of the zoo gardens!

By this time, I was approaching 15 years, the school leaving age. My father was strongly against working at the zoo, which had been a wish of mine from a very small boy. He felt that it would be a dead end job with no future in it. Having nobody with whom to discuss this, I decided to speak to the veterinary surgeon that had treated Bobby a few months earlier. I managed to get an appointment with him eventually, and I found to my amazement that Mr. Courtney was a Consultant Veterinary Surgeon at Regents Park Zoo. He informed and warned me of the arduous work involved in working within the zoo. This would include long hours, low pay, heavy physical work, much studying and little time left for pleasure. Despite all this I had decided that for me it would be a pleasure to work there.

Having left school, my first port of call was the offices of London Zoo to enquire about work as a trainee keeper. I was introduced to the gardenís executive, Les Flewin, who informed me of the long waiting list they had of young people who wanted to work with animals and that my chances of employment were nil. This was due to the fact that many relatives of the present staff wanted jobs and that they were most likely to be appointed to any vacant positions.

I decided that the way I would deal with this would be to pay regular visits on a daily basis to Mr. Flewin! Everyday I waited in the foyer of the main office for his arrival. I pestered him, asking, "Is there any chance of work?" He replied with a smile on his face, "Sorry son". This continued for a month.

On one of these visits he invited me, surprisingly, into his office. He said, "Son, you are a most persistent lad. You can start in the pheasantry on Monday!" Nobody could have been more surprised than me. I had arrived!

The author as a helper outside the Birds of Prey Aviaries at the beginning of his carrer. (PA)

CHAPTER 2
"From Pheasantry to Royalty"

Monday morning came and I went to the timekeeper's gate to be met by the Head Keeper of the pheasantry - Mr. Simpson. He took me to the pheasantry, introduced me to the other staff and told me the long hours I would be working - possibly an eleven hour day with only one week-end off in seven, with one day off a week! The pay would be £3.00 a week for this. I learnt that my duties would include cleaning out many cages and aviaries. I was also taught food preparation, which involved mixing various seeds, corn, biscuits and vitamins in buckets. I also had to cut up the meat for the owls and other meat-eaters.

The Head Keeper of the North Mammal House, Mr. Audice, used to take a large husky for a walk in the zoo grounds. Sometimes Chappie, the husky, would go his own way, wandering down to where I was preparing food for the birds. Growling alternately from me to the meat he looked on the cutting up board, before taking what he fancied. I just stood there helplessly wondering what to do. He would walk out of the kitchen, smiling. That's how it seemed to me!

Eventually the bird overseer informed me that I was to be transferred to the birdhouse. The Head-Keeper, Mr. Newson, was an ex-Naval man, who had apparently won the war on his own! At 08.00 hours we would be lined up in the Mess Room when he would get his boson's whistle from the locker. On blowing it, we would have to march out in file to our work for the day. The first job of the day was to collect all the water bowls and dishes from the cages and aviaries, to be washed and cleaned and put on the hot water pipes to dry in the bird house.

On one occasion, I was feeling very hungry and helped myself to one of the birds' bananas. Not wanting to be caught, I sat in the toilet to eat it and proceeded to flush the skin down the toilet! I later discovered the Head-Keeper had found the skin floating in the bottom of the toilet and an enquiry followed. I admitted the offence and was taken for disciplining to

John with Rab, the cheetah from the North Mammal House. (PA)

Mexican hairless bitch with offspring, which gave me such pleasure as a lad. (PA)

the curator, Mr. Yelling, who reminded me that the food was for the birds and not for human consumption!

Two days later, whilst working in the aviary with the senior keeper, I was asked to turn on the water to the small pond. The tap appearing to be bent, I proceeded to straighten it, resulting in a fracture to the main pipe. I was instructed by a senior keeper to report this incident to the Head Keeper. After searching, I found Mr. Newson eating a banana. Not commenting on this, I told him what had happened to the main pipe. His reply was that this was the third such pipe to have been broken that week by me and I should work in an area with no water! Later in the week, while I was washing the bird tins in the kitchen and Mr. Newson was preparing the bird food, I strolled over and openly helped myself to a banana. I unzipped and consumed it. Looking at me in amazement he said "Upstairs!" We had reached the bottom of the stairs when I said "Are we going to tell Mr. Yelling about the banana that you consumed?" We immediately changed direction and returned to the kitchen. Nothing further was said, but from that day I was given an occasional banana!

Attached to the birdhouse were the Humming birds. On special occasions I was allowed to go with the senior keeper to help out. This was very specialised work, which involved preparation of a very special diet in liquid form. This was put into glass feeding tubes and suspended from the branches so the birds could hover and feed on the wing.

As time went on, the Humming bird house was converted into a tropical walk through aviary. At one time a succession of dead birds were found on the aviary floor. The result of a post-mortem examination concluded that they had been shot by a pistol or air rifle. The local Police suggested that they should observe during the opening hours of the zoo, through a one-way mirror. Eventually the culprit was apprehended and, through the process of law, was dealt with accordingly.

I learnt a great deal whilst working with the Humming birds about their behaviour, feeding habits and courtship. The smallest of the Humming birds are the tiny ones in the West Indies, Cuban Bee Hummer, the smallest bird known at $2^{1}/_{4}$ inches from the tip of its bill to the tip of its tail. Its body is the size of a large bumblebee and weighs less than 2 grams. The largest, on the other hand, is the $8^{1}/_{2}$ inch Giant Humming bird of the high Andes, which weighs approximately 20 grams. It is one of the few that flaps its wings slowly enough for them to be seen in flight.

Regardless of normal duties, all employees except the aquarium, reptile and insect staff helped with rides for children on the main square in the zoo. These would commence at 13.45 hours and terminate at 15.45 hours and included elephant, llama, donkey, pony, pony and trap and camel rides. According to one's grade, one would be detailed to the elephants or donkeys! I often had to collect a donkey from the children's zoo and take him to the riding area, having brushed and cleaned the animal first.

On one occasion, the duty overseer of the day arrived on the square - one could say well under the influence of alcohol. He said to me "I will

9

show you how to drive this trap properly." Going off at quite a pace, encountering a curve as it went around the flowerbed with the moat on the other side, he lost control. Consequently the back wheel ended up in the moat! The ponies had to be unharnessed and returned to the children's zoo with the trap while the overseer had to be carried to his office to sleep for some considerable time. The following day the Director of the zoo, Mr. Rawlings DFC, OBE, asked for a statement regarding the incident. Asking if the overseer was inebriated, I said "Oh no, he was just unwell!" He accepted this explanation but we both knew it to be untrue.

Over the next two years, I continued to work in the birdhouse. On one occasion we were told that a VIP was coming and we were to keep out of the way for two hours, being placed in the remotest part of the birdhouse. While occupying ourselves washing down the paintwork, the door suddenly opened and in walked HRH The Duke of Edinburgh. Before we could say or do anything he said, "So this is where you lads are working, I see." He was pursued immediately by the red-faced officials who stood there silently to attention while he continued to address us. It seemed like hours but it was only minutes. It was apparent to me from this first meeting with The Duke of Edinburgh that he had a very keen interest in wildlife in general. From this time onwards he was to have a greater involvement in the Zoological Society and wildlife worldwide.

During this period in the bird house, I recall a young lady by the name of Jane who used to come into the kitchen with her Bush Baby called "Boozie" to collect food for it. This girl eventually became famous as Jane Goodall the authority on chimpanzees, having spent many years in Africa studying their behavioural patterns.

CHAPTER 3
"Fish and Bones"

Having now worked for two years in the birdhouse, I felt I wanted to broaden my horizons. I discussed this with the Head Keeper who said he would speak with the overseer of birds, Jack Gregory. It transpired that a vacancy had arisen on the Diving Birds and Birds of Prey Section, which also included waterfowl, wading birds, sea birds, penguins, birds of the crow family and flamingos. With all these varieties of birds, it would be a challenging experience.

I was told that I could transfer to the Diving Birds Section the following week, to work under the father of the man who was in charge of me in the bird house. I was to work here for the next seven years, accompanied by a lot of studying and reading on the many varieties of birds. I also spent countless hours asking my superiors questions on feeding, behaviour and breeding, for I found this was an invaluable way to gain knowledge from their experience. It was about this time that I used to borrow money from my grandmother to purchase second hand books on birds in general.

Having changed to this section, I took on the typical duties of a junior helper from breaking up frozen fish to scrubbing out pens and cages. Some of these cages contained large Birds of Prey. A Crowned Hawk Eagle would attack me on sight, flying at my face with its talons extended. I would have to stick a broom up between me and the bird for protection as I passed between the cages. This Crowned Hawk Eagle only really respected its regular keeper.

This was not the last encounter with these raptors! I admit I had been advised to wear a hat but, being an obstinate lad, I thought I knew it all and did not need to wear one and paid the price. So on another occasion a Stellers Sea Eagle flew across the aviary and, closing its talons, banged me on the head.

Part of my training was to learn the procedure for catching such an eagle by cornering the bird and offering a broom head for it to grab. One had to make sure that it clutched it with both its powerful talons, enabling one to catch it by the legs nearer the body. This was the standard routine for immobilising a bird for inspection by the veterinary officer who checked for overgrown beaks or talons as well as on some occasions for sexing.

I was also taught how to make jessies. These are straps which are put on each leg of the bird, with a swivel attachment, enabling us to take the bird to functions, on our own, during members' evenings in the zoo restaurant. One of my favourite Birds of Prey for such events was the Verreaux's Eagle. This African bird is blackish-grey in colour with a wing span of approximately eight feet - extremely tame and friendly and therefore easy to handle, allowing me to stroke it.

One morning I was detailed, on arrival at work at 08.00 hours, to go with the Head Keeper to the Three Island Pond where flamingos were housed. There were Greater, Rosy, Lesser and Chilean flamingos. The first duty on arrival at any section in the zoo was to check for any dead, sick or injured animals. Any dead ones went to the post-mortem area, while sick or injured were either seen in situ or transported to the veterinary hospital for further examination. In the summer period the flamingos could go in and out of their shed to the pond area as they wished. However, in the winter months, these birds would have to be coaxed back into their shed at nightfall because the pond would freeze, trapping the bird's thin legs beneath the ice.

One winter's evening a colleague of mine, Matthew Hennessy, was asked to go round to the Three Island Pond to open the valve to drain the flamingo pond. Unbeknown to Matthew, the works department had detailed a bricklayer, earlier in the day, to brick up the inside of the manhole, thinking that the pond would not be in use. On opening the valve, Matthew submerged the Polish bricklayer in three feet of water. On returning, Matthew reported to me that some man was making funny noises in the manhole. The following morning, expecting some repercussions from the incident the night before, nothing was said about it, to our great relief!

The diet of the day, which I had to make up under supervision, was brown bread soaked in water, with wheat to which the correct amount of carrot oil had been added. This was given to the flamingos as a colouring additive for their plumage via plastic buckets, enabling the birds to sieve

Author and eagle in the aviary. (FK)

through it with their bills. Sometimes we would add crushed shrimps and fishmeal to their meal. The overall daily requirements for the section would be fish, meat, some vegetables, mice, rats and locusts. The great variety of food was due to the fact that we had so many bird species. I also made nests out of mud and clay, hopefully encouraging the birds to breed. Unfortunately, sadly, this did not happen during my time with them.

One morning at about 08.30 hours, while on my way to the penguins with the Head Keeper, we passed the reptile house and heard a terrific commotion coming from the animals inside. We entered to find six men lying face down in a hole. At this point in time, we did not realise what had happened. I pulled the top one off whom I recognised to be Tony Hodges, a keeper who worked in the reptile house. Having gained the Bronze Cross in Life Saving in my school days, I immediately administered artificial respiration for some time. He then started to vomit all over me, which I recognised as a good sign. It seemed like a lifetime before the emergency services arrived and finally took over. We were later told that five of the men were dead on arrival at hospital, but the one whom I had worked on was still alive at this time. He remained in a coma however for 11 months until he eventually died.

It transpired that an artesian well, which was undergoing inspection by workmen two days previously, had been covered over by sacks and cordoned off by a barrier. Apparently gas had built up during the weekend and when the workmen removed the sacks they were overcome by the gas fumes and collapsed. The keepers' involvement was in trying to help the workmen. Some months later I was awarded a commendation from The Royal Humane Society for skill shown in trying to save the life of a man.

This incident delayed my introduction to the penguin pool. On arrival there, George Newson went through all the cleaning procedures, which involved cleaning the pond and chlorinating it twice weekly to kill off algae and bacteria in the pond. As George was showing me around, we passed the adjacent pens of the Lower Mappin Terrace which housed Big-Horned Sheep, Wild Boar, Peccaries and Vicunas. One of the latter grabbed my collar and then proceeded to spit regurgitated food all over my face. George just laughed and said "Part of the course, lad!" To which I replied "I'll stink now!" "Nothing to what you will later when we start cutting up and gutting the herrings!"

Feeding time at the Birds of Prey aviaries. (FK)

Feeding the King Penguins under the supervision of George Newson, Head Keeper. (FK)

That afternoon I was to accompany him on the public feeds for the penguins. I was flabbergasted to watch the King Penguins take about thirteen whole herrings, while the others darted about in the water as George threw the fish in all directions, making a display for the public.

Suddenly, one of the Gentoo penguins came out of the water at great speed, in the air and, misjudging a small tree, landed between its branches. George went over to the stricken penguin, finding its head stuck in the fork of the tree; he released it and returned it to the water! It appeared to be none the worse for wear from this escapade. On the second or third occasion, George allowed me to feed them myself. Picking up a herring out of the pail I thought I would try to throw the fish much further than George! This I managed to do but, unfortunately losing my balance, much to the amusement of the public I joined the penguins in the pool! Matters were made worse by the fact that I was in my best bib and tucker!

One morning, after cleaning out the penguin pool behind the lion house, I thought I would pop along to look at the big cats. Being near teatime, there was no one on duty in the house. The tools were just laid near each cage. Picking up a tennis bass broom, with outstretched arm I offered it to a large male lion! To my amazement he grabbed the broom head and, his claws ripping it apart, he caused me to fall backwards holding just the handle. There was no way I could retrieve the broom head so I got out of there as quickly as possible! Later, as George and I were on our way to the penguin pool, he stopped to speak to Mr. Hitchcock, the Head Keeper of the Lion House. He went on to tell him that some prat had given one of the lions a broom head and he would love to catch the little sod! Neither of these men, or anyone else, knew my secret. Needless to say I had learnt my lesson and never did this again.

As time went by I was to spend more time on the Birds of Prey. One morning while cleaning out the Condor enclosure, I was asked a question by a man of the cloth, who was accompanying a school party. His question to me was "Do the inmates ever attack you?" Being a cheeky lad, I replied, holding up my broom "No Sir, my rod and staff do comfort me!" It wasn't long afterwards that I found myself in front of the establishment's officer. He informed me that the Vicar who had spoken to me earlier that day had reported me. With a smile on my face I said, "You mean to say he reported me, the old so-and-so!" "Yes" said the officer. "You must take this as a warning, and conduct yourself correctly in the presence of the public".

Another time when I thought I might be up for disciplining was when I was pursuing one of my colleagues with an iron spike, endeavouring to poke him with it, in a friendly way of course. As we turned a corner, with me in hot pursuit, we nearly collided with Major General Dalton, the zoo director, who just looked in amazement. Daily, for many weeks, I waited to be summoned to the offices. However, this never happened. On my way back from lunch another day, I walked straight into the man himself, General Dalton. He said, "I have always been meaning to ask you if you ever caught that chap!" This was not the last time I was to come into contact with the powers that be!

On another occasion, having taken an electric zoo vehicle from outside the canteen, I proceeded to have a joy ride around the zoo. I first encountered a large hole at the rear of the lion house, which workmen had made but I eventually managed, with my friend Matthew, to manhandle it out. At this point, Matthew had had enough and decided to walk back to our area of work. Whilst returning the vehicle I then passed the Birds of Prey, and to my amazement, Mr. Flewin, the Garden's executive, was coming towards me in his Oxford Cambridge. Having not seen me at first, he swerved into the wall. Getting out of his car he came over to enquire if I was all right. Expecting the worst, I was flabbergasted when he said to me "Entirely my fault, I did not see you." He never did ask what I was doing driving a dustcart, unauthorised!

One of my tasks was to go each morning to the canteen to collect George's coffee. On returning I used to find him tuned into his radio listening to the Clitheroe Kid, in the Mess Room. We had to respect George's wish for quietness during the programme, as he sat there smoking his No.3 cigarettes!

During our tea break, there was a knock on the door one day and it was the overseer, Jack Ward, on one of his routine visits. He had come to ask George when it would be convenient for collection of some flamingos from Buckingham Palace gardens. These birds were to be housed at London Zoo for the winter months and George asked me to accompany him on this occasion.

This, for me, was an interesting opportunity to see inside the Palace grounds and also to see how the birds were moved in hessian boxes so that they did not damage themselves during transit. They were placed in a large wooden building, adjacent to the Three Island Pond, which was deeply littered with peat to keep their feet warm during the cold weather. They were returned to Buckingham Palace in the spring but this was not to be my last encounter with the Royals.

At about this time, Mr. Newson Senior was due for retirement, when he would be able to spend more time at his beloved Arsenal Football Club. His successor was to be Ernie Scrivener, who was an ex-SAS soldier from the Second World War. He was ruddy-faced, of medium build and of a quiet disposition. One never knew what he was thinking and, as a consequence, never really got to know him well. One minute he would seem to have the patience of Job and the next undergo a complete character change, becoming most irascible. This, I was told, was probably due to his war time experience. Despite this, he was a most likeable and knowledgeable person.

Adjacent to the Mess Room was a holding area for crates and bird boxes. This area was cleared for Matthew and myself to have our three or four daily boxing rounds! These were always friendly contests with my Irish friend, who spent more time in my home than his own. One day Mr. Scrivener suggested that I might like to use up some of my energy in a more constructive way by becoming a member of the 21st SAS Territorial Army Regiment, of which he was a member.

Consequently, a few weeks later, I was called for an interview for the Regiment. Later I was told I had been selected, which was a great privilege and boost to my esteem. The arduous training that I was to receive was to prove invaluable for projects in the years to come.

One task, which was to test Mr. Scrivener's patience and endurance, was to recapture Goldie, the Golden Eagle that had flown out past the keeper as he entered the cage one sunny morning. This received extensive cover by the media. Goldie would swoop down onto small dogs being exercised by their owners in Regents Park. On one occasion an elderly lady was seen fending off the pursuer by lashing out with her umbrella. Eventually, Goldie's freedom from the open blue skies ended with his recapture to rejoin his mate, only for him to escape again two weeks later. For a second time he was recaptured.

It was about this time that I was to meet my future wife, Sheila, who had a seasonal appointment working as a hostess in the children's zoo. During my regular task of cleaning out the penguin pool, she would stop to speak to me on her way to work, not always getting a polite response! This was not due to her behaviour but my own. At the end of the season she left the Society to work elsewhere for the winter months, but was to re-apply the following spring for a position in the children's zoo. I continued to see her regularly at work but at this time she had a regular boyfriend.

My mother had often enquired about my work at the zoo, showing a keen interest. I suggested that she should come to the Park with a friend on my complimentary tickets. So, one Sunday afternoon, I met her and her friend at the zoo gates, having permission from my Head Keeper to have an hour to show them around. Our first port of call was the lion house of which my mother was very nervous, because we were going behind the scenes, where she was to be shown how the animals were moved from inside to outside cages via tunnels. Having seen enough she was pleasantly surprised to be offered a nice cup of sweet tea by the Head Keeper, to calm her troubled nerves! Whilst admiring the rug under the table in the Mess Room within inches of her feet, it suddenly arose and walked out of the room into the passageway - the rug being a half grown, hand-reared tiger which, being quite tame, it was common to see in the nursery area. My mother, nearly dropping her cup of tea, looked at me and said, "You little sod - you knew about this all the time!" Her speechless friend was also petrified. Needless to say my mother did not come for a return visit, but continued to tell people what I had done to her. The lion house staff found all this most amusing.

With the introduction of the Keepers' course, I was required to attend many lectures and practical periods over the next two years by the Educational Department. At the end of this there were written examinations and oral interviews by a panel of veterinary surgeons and zoologists. Having satisfied the Examinations Board, I was awarded The Society's Diploma in Care and Management of Animals. This I received from Lord Zucherman, The President of the Society, in the main offices of the zoo.

One of the most important exercises was the weekly animal escape procedure. Keepers had to report to designated areas whilst other keepers would ensure safety of the public by locking them in the houses until the all clear. These actions would take the form of nets being dropped over the tunnels to keep the escaped animals in a confined area. Senior members of staff would be on standby with immobilising guns if required.

On one occasion, I was requested by the Garden's Executive to come in on my day off to play the part of the escaped animal, which was to be a carnivore. The staff had to identify and track me down, having received a

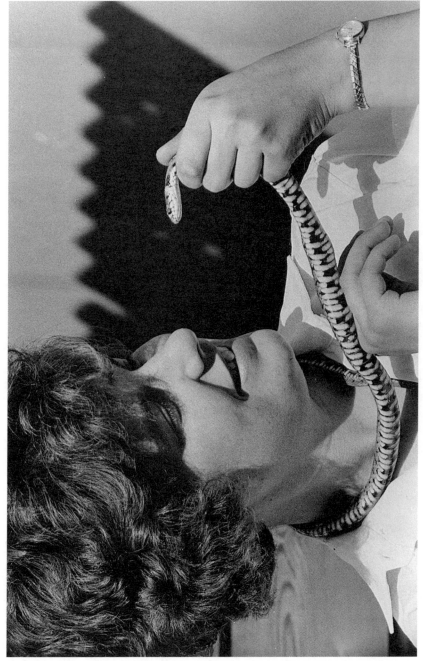

Sheila, my wife to be, working in the Children's Zoo. (DT)

description of the beast, which was me in white overalls! No tiger suits in those days! After much chasing and no luck by my pursuers I decided to rest upon some rafters under the Mappin Terraces, watching my pursuers below! After two hours I surrendered. If nothing else it was a morning's overtime!

My next encounter with a member of the Royal Family was the Duke of Edinburgh who was again coming for a tour around the zoo. I was selected, with Mr. Macory, to walk in front of the Duke to clear the way ahead and open doors. This lasted for some hours, at the end of which the zoo officials politely dismissed us, but after we had only walked a few yards away the Duke recalled us. I looked at Joe and said, "What have we done now?" As we approached the Duke he enquired where we were going. We replied "Back to work Sir." He said "Oh no, if you can walk before me all day you can certainly join me for tea." This was to the embarrassment of all the zoo officials, particularly when the Duke seated us either side of him at the table with our cucumber sandwiches!

My first encounter, in a small way, with elephants was through loading children on for rides in the main square of the zoo. This might happen once or twice a week. One particular Asian elephant had a nasty habit of transferring its weight against the steps on which the keeper stood to load children onto the howdah and, in so doing, it pushed the steps over and the keeper with them. This brought strong verbal response from the elephant handler to check it. These rides did not continue for very long as, on one occasion, an elephant with children on board bolted through a tunnel, returning to its house with the keeper in hot pursuit! It was decided to discontinue elephant rides after this incident.

On summer mornings I would often walk from St. John's Wood where I lived, crossing Regents Park to the zoo. One particular morning, I had stopped by the lake to watch the waterfowl when something in the grass caught my eye. Bending down I was to discover a baby kestrel, which had fallen, presumably, out of its nest. I took it to work and asked the advice of Mr. Macory on how I could go about rearing it. I took the kestrel daily to work and home with me in the evenings.

Kessie became very friendly and tame over the year, living on the veranda of my parents' home, much to the amusement of passers by, who would often stop and enquire what the bird was. I fed Kessie on mice, locusts, earthworms and any insects I could find. I trained her to come on

The author with Kessie, the Kestrel, now fully mature. (Fr)

to my arm when I called and would reward her with titbits, such as meat. She used to sleep on the wooden framework of my bed at night, facing me. I had to ensure there was newspaper on the floor beneath her! This did not continue for long, as my father informed me that my bedroom was not a menagerie and the bird should live outside. So I told him that he would have to make Kessie a cage. This he did.

Sheila, of whom I spoke earlier, was to become an important part of my life for it was at about this time that I proposed to her. She went on holiday to Spain and on her return she gave me her answer. We were to be married the following year in St. Luke's Church, Enfield by Father Bale, who was Sheila's family priest and friend. We went on honeymoon to Sheila's Aunt and Uncle in North Devon.

CHAPTER 4
"Work with Mammals Now Begins"

After spending seven years on the Diving Birds and Birds of Prey, I felt that it was time to broaden my experience with other animals. I noticed an advertisement for a Grade 4 Keeper in the North Mammal House. This was a very sought after area in which to work, with many medium sized cats and canines. My overseer at this time pointed out that Mr. Aldis was a very strict disciplinarian. He wondered whether our personalities would clash. However, having known Mr. Aldis since my first days at the zoo, I believed that I would have a lot to learn from him and considered this a good move. I applied for the post as Junior Keeper and to my amazement I was offered the job.

On my first day in the North Mammal House one of my duties was to polish all the seventy brass padlocks on the cages. Mr. Aldis presented me with reference books on species within the house and ordered me to read up the information in these books as in the near future he would be quizzing me on it. I had to call him "Mr. Aldis" at all times as did even the senior staff who had been there for some years.

One of the routines that Mr. Aldis was most keen on was the weekly examination of dung and urine samples, to check the animals' general condition. These were collected by the keepers, for Mr. Aldis' inspection. One of the common ailments was hairballs due to constant cleaning and licking by the animals. This was treated with a dose of liquid paraffin, but if there was anything he was not sure about he would ask for further examination by the pathology laboratory.

One of my responsibilities was to clean out the outside public viewing cages. This had to be achieved by 10.00 a.m., the time of the first public admittance to the grounds. A keeper would unlock the cage whilst I performed this task and then lock up after me, until after six months I was allocated my personal keys. During this period of time I was only allowed to do the most menial tasks required of a Junior Keeper. Gradually, once I

Rab the Cheetah stretches for a tit-bit. (Fr)

Majestic pose of a fully-grown cheetah in Regent's Park Zoo. (Fr)

had gained the confidence of my superiors, I was given varying tasks, one of which was to crate up a male cheetah for overseas departure whilst Mr. Aldis was at a meeting.

I was a little worried to say the least but, having checked and double-checked that everything was in place, with great relief I was able to get the cheetah into the crate without any problem.

I finally felt that I was on the way to becoming a keeper in my own small way and as the months went by, I was left on my own to make decisions of some importance and move animals about the building on my own. However, it is easy to become over-confident! On one occasion I was letting out the Asiatic Wild Dog, forgetting that I had previously released the European Wild Cat. These animals were now outside in the cages together! Waiting for a noise which never came, I decided to walk around to the outside enclosure to see what was going on, only to discover that they were sitting and looking at each other. So I quickly went back inside and opened the sliding door to let the Wild Dog back in. This he did willingly! Needless to say, I have never divulged this to anyone to this day!

On another occasion, probably due to lack of concentration, I assumed that when I was letting two leopards out into the outside enclosure they had walked out together. On entering the cage, to clean it out, I was amazed to find, as I stood up, a large tail dangling in front of my eyes. For probably seconds, but which seemed like hours, I remained motionless - gathering my thoughts. With as much pretence of normality as I could muster, I slowly turned back towards the entrance. On arrival at the door, without a backward glance I stepped outside and shut it as quickly as I could, with the leopard lying on the log above, watching me! This frightening experience was a lesson for the future - to remember to check and double check - which I was to imprint on the minds of all junior keepers.

At about this time I was approaching my eleventh year with the Society when Colin Rawlings, the Director of the Society, suggested, that I might like to go and work at Whipsnade Park Zoo in Bedfordshire. He asked me to give this some thought. I discussed this with Sheila, my wife, and, as we were expecting our first baby, we felt that the countryside might be a good place in which to bring up children. I decided to ask my overseer at this time whether he considered it to be an advantageous career move. He told me that the North Mammal House, where I currently worked, was due for demolition in the near future and that a new education block was due to be built there. He also informed me that my relocation with the Society could be anywhere within the menagerie. I therefore arranged an appointment with Mr. Rawlings to tell him that I was interested in the new post at Whipsnade. He said he would inform the Director, Mr. Tong, that I would like to be interviewed and to see the accommodation which went with the post.

A date was fixed and the Society arranged for myself and Sheila to be chauffeur driven from London to Whipsnade. The interview, which took place in the main office, was successful. The Zoo, being somewhat like the Army, asked where I would like to work. I requested the Bird Section and was promptly told that I would be with the elephants. My immediate inward thought was "Oh shit," having heard many stories over the years from people working with pachyderms. As I was a thick-skinned Homo sapiens, maybe we would be compatible! We went back to London to think about our possible future at Whipsnade and, in particular, to discuss my offer with Mr. Rawlings. After a lot of thought about the new job, and swayed by the presence of a six months old new addition to the family, Rachel, we decided to embark on this new venture.

CHAPTER 5
"Training starts with a Bump"

So, in April 1968, with the help of London Zoo's transport department, we loaded up in Enfield onto an open topped lorry and set I off with our driver, Arthur Payne, to the wilds of Bedfordshire. Sheila and baby Rachel arrived some hours later in her parents' car.

After a few days to settle in, I reported to the timekeeper's office and was met by an overseer, who I later found out to be Mr. Gladman, the brother of the owner of the local village shop in Studham. He took me to the elephant house where I was introduced to the Head Keeper, Charlie Bailey, his second in charge, John Datlin, and the keeper Brian Rodgers.

Charlie took me and introduced me to the elephants. The oldest Asian one, Mangal Peary, had discarded her last set of teeth and her diet consisted of chaff, which was easily digested. The other adult Asian elephant was Vallie, who had not the best of temperaments and was not very kindly disposed to new keepers! She had been hand reared by Mr. Gladman and so only just tolerated everyone else. The rest of the herd was made up of four Asian and three Africans, the smallest Asian being Min. Katie, Msmava and Metdere were the Africans and Kumara was the mischievous Asian.

For the first weeks I worked with the young elephants that were being bottle-fed every four hours on FMS powdered milk. Various other types of milk had been tried unsuccessfully - for example, Jersey cream, pasteurised milk and skimmed milk. After a great deal of experimentation powdered milk was found to be the most palatable when given at blood temperature. Gradually lucerne and some cooked rice were introduced into the diet.

On some occasions the milk would be rejected, either being the wrong temperature or texture. This sometimes caused scouring, which brought on diarrhoea, and the veterinary surgeon had to be consulted. The problem could eventually be rectified with a change of diet or

The herd of Elephants at Whipsnade Zoo, early 1970's. (LZ)

modification. One of the veterinarians often called was a Mr. Senior from Dunstable, who had a wealth of experience with elephants.

It was about this time that I was introduced to the training methods of the baby elephants. One of the first things that they were taught was to lie down on command, achieved over many weeks through arduous and painstaking work. Firstly the elephant was tethered on all fours. One at a time each hind leg was slowly pulled out by a keeper until the animal would go down onto its haunches. Having achieved this, the two keepers on the front legs would go through the same process. During this time there would be much bellowing and lashing out by the animals, resulting in keepers being thrown across the stable and acquiring many bruises - to the hilarity of the watching public, who would often report us to the main office for, what they saw as, cruelty. What the public did not fully comprehend was that thorough training was a necessary pre-requisite to controlling the animals, for the safety of staff and for veterinary visits. Naturally enough, if an animal would stand still on command, it was much easier when treatment was required. The elephants were also taught to put a foot onto a log. This was an obvious advantage when routine foot care was needed.

The elephants were also trained to come on command. Sometimes, they would change from an amble to a charge, hitting one in the midriff and bowling one over! If hit in a certain area, this could prove to be rather painful! Again the public would find this most amusing, especially if the keeper landed in a pile of dung on his backside, which often happened during training - Charlie Bailey, the Head Keeper, would comment "You're not an elephant keeper until you have had a few knocks, boy."

Sadly, at about this time, one of the baby elephants, Min, was found to have a heart defect and died. It was not long after this that Mangal Peary died of old age, so we were down to five elephants.

In the following weeks the Head Keeper resigned after twenty years service. John Datlin was promoted to Head Keeper and I was asked to take the position of second in charge. I felt very apprehensive about this due to the fact that I had no control over the large Asian elephant, Vallie. In the following weeks we needed to gradually introduce the young elephants to her. This took place in the main compound adjacent to the elephant house. The baby elephants were led out into the paddock to meet Vallie, whose greeting was not friendly, but with a word from John Datlin she would

Mangal Peary and Vallie watching over the baby elephants Katie and Kumara. (Fr)

come under control. As part of the exercise, John would exit the compound, leaving me alone with the group. It did not take long before Vallie realised that she was without her Head Keeper, so she made tracks towards me. To avoid being grabbed by her I would dodge between the trees. It seemed like hours before John returned, but in fact it was only minutes. Again a few words from him were enough to make her change direction and return to normal feeding. However, at the slightest opportunity, she would take advantage if she thought nobody was watching and try and push one of the baby elephants into the moat or pond, causing abrasions and bruising to the babies. Consequently, the gradual process of introduction was most time consuming, as there would have to be a member of staff in or around the paddock all day long. But over this period I was gradually building up an excellent rapport with the babies and particularly Kumara. She was a playful and mischievous character, looking for any opportunity to either run off with a broom or shovel and always having the last word with a grunt or groan!

As mentioned earlier, the young elephants were fed every four hours around the clock, which included late night and early morning feeds. It was important from day one that as far as possible we kept to the same keepers for these tasks. When this was not possible it sometimes had a bad effect on the animals, resulting in refusal to feed, causing a setback in their progress.

The rapport between the animals continued to grow over the next two years. The position with Vallie had, however, not improved much. One of the problems was getting her into the stable at night after John had gone home. She would enter the stable, start to feed, and then turning on a penny would rush towards me as I was trying to close the door, hitting the door with the side of her head and re-opening it before I could put the locking bolt in position. After some thought and some bruised knees sustained from going though the barrier at great speed with a three-ton elephant in pursuit, I decided that I must re-position the evening feed of fruit and vegetables so that the animal's manoeuvrability was restricted, giving me a few extra seconds in which to close the door! It's amazing what you can perfect if you have an incentive! Vallie's disposition towards me did not change until John Datlin's transfer in 1971 to Head Keeper of the Bird Section.

The baby elephant, Kumara seen through Vallie's legs. (LZ)

Having read all I could find on the management and training of elephants, I eventually decided I would try and win her over by reducing her intake of food and sitting for hours in front of her, calling her to come to me and then, but only then, offering her some tasty morsel. Using this method, within six months, I could not only go in with Vallie, but she would also obey some of my commands. This growing rapport with Vallie enabled me to be in the compound with all the elephants with greater confidence. She would now lie down on command and come when called, which was a tremendous improvement.

In my capacity as Head Keeper I was given a Senior Keeper, Colin Mew, from the Bird Section. He was to remain with me for twenty years. However most of the junior members of staff came and went with monotonous regularity - lack of determination, stamina and interest and sometimes an understandable fear of large animals would unnerve inexperienced keepers. This would be particularly apparent during the winter months, when the animals would be in the confined area of their eighteen-foot square stables. These keepers would never be allowed in the stables on their own and it was always drummed into them to stay in the centre of the area and not between the elephant and the wall.

The elephants would deliberately, on occasions, speed up their movement around the keepers, obviously trying to unnerve them. I told the men to stay with me and continue working normally. However, more often than not, they would await their opportunity and dive through the bars to safety. This behaviour proved to be aimed at the trainees, for, as soon as the keeper had left, the animal's actions returned to normal. This made the re-introduction of staff more difficult the following day.

At about this time, I was approached by the park's policeman to see if I would be interested in becoming a member of the Special Constabulary. He often visited me when I was feeding the young elephants, during the night, when he was on his rounds. After some thought I decided that this would be a valuable experience and provide an interest outside work. However I had to have permission from the Curator to be allowed time off work to appear in court, if needed. I was to spend seven years in the Special Constabulary, rising to rank of Inspector.

There were many amusing incidents to which I was called. One of those, which comes to mind, was when we received a call over the radio to an evening function at the zoo! One of the guests had decided to streak

Youngsters at play with sand and log in the compound. (LZ)

around the Dolphinarium. On arrival he was found to be partly re-clothed but somewhat inebriated. After a few words, we proceeded on our way!

Another incident that occurred, whilst on duty in the Whipsnade district, involved a lady motorist who had failed to obey the stop sign. Approaching her, I became aware that the occupant of the vehicle was the zoo Curator's wife. At this point she had not recognised me. I found out at a later date that the penny had dropped!

The new chimpanzee house, which had been under construction for some time, was nearing completion and I was informed that this would come under my control. Initially the chimpanzee house was to be stocked with ex-tea party chimps from London Zoo. There was Winnie, Daisy, Roo, Primrose, China and one male, Rasdas.

It was not uncommon to call upon the works department to repair the weld mesh, which the chimps could break by fabricating ropes out of their bedding which was made out of wood wool. The chimps would first plait it into a length of rope and then soak it in the water from the drinking pipe. They would then tie this around the welds and constantly pull until the weld broke. Using their faeces they would smear this around the broken weld to disguise it. Consequently, the cage would have to be examined daily. Another favourite pastime of the chimps was to constantly rattle the main cage door until eventually the Yale lock would break. So every two to three months the locks had to be replaced.

It was very important to count the chimps out from their night quarters to the outside enclosure before cleaning out their sleeping dens. On one occasion a chimp was discovered asleep under the bedding. Fortunately, the door was not completely opened so no harm was done. However, anyone who may have entered to clean up would have encountered a grown chimp that could have caused serious injury.

It was essential that one did not wear any loose clothing or, in the case of young ladies, have loose hair, as the chimps could easily grab hair or clothes as one walked by. This happened to my second in charge on one occasion when China, a large female, grabbed a piece of wool from his sleeve and continued alone the tunnel unravelling the sweater to the shoulder until I could cut it. These antics were always of great amusement to the public and, of course, the T.V unit!

Returning to the elephant house, we had an on-going problem with a large Asian elephant that had not passed a motion for twenty-six days. As

Primrose an ex tea party chimp with her offspring. (LZ)

Baby chimp. (LZ)

one can imagine the animal's circumference had enlarged considerably due to the gases building up in her body. So, I summoned the veterinary officer who turned up in a suit. His words to me were "Hot water, fairy liquid, stirrup pump." I said, "Yes." He said, "Well, get them then." This I did, saying, "Are you going to change out of your suit?" No words passed his lips as he prepared to administer the soapy water into the rear of the animal. I proceeded to the other end! I informed him that I would steady the animal. He made no comment! Within a few moments I could hear some gurgling noises coming from the rear end. Suddenly there was an enormous explosion. I walked round to where the vet was and he looked like a representative from Cadbury's, being covered in very wet dung from head to foot! Needless to say he was not amused and left the scene forthwith. The elephant appeared to have a smile on her face, like that of her Head Keeper's!

On another occasion a young keeper was given the simple task of watering the elephants, only to return to say that Kumara had taken the bucket and smashed it to pieces. My comment to him was "It's only a bucket!" He replied "There's more to it than that. She has also torn away half the pipe-work from the tap!"

The elephants are now fast approaching six years of age and consequently beginning to develop individual characteristics, particularly Kumara, who would take advantage of any young trainee and take the broom, shovel, wheelbarrow, or anything from him or her, smashing them with great enjoyment. Katie, the African, needed a much quieter approach as she was very nervy and one would have to let her know of one's arrival by speaking to her in a very gentle way, otherwise she would spin round with her ears out in alarm. This also applied to Msmava and to Mentende who went to Edinburgh Zoological Gardens for an extended holiday. She travelled there in a crate, on the back of a low-loader, waving to everyone on the motorway with her trunk!

Sadly, on one of my days off, I was to learn that Msmava had received a fatal blow to the chest whilst sparring with Katie in the compound, and had died from a massive haemorrhage. The post-mortem revealed that there was probably a weakness at the area where the blow was received. Katie had tried desperately to revive Msmava by attempting to pick her up, but in vain. Observers in the wild have noted such behaviour.

Katie, the placid African cow and Kumara, the mischievous Asian cow. (FP)

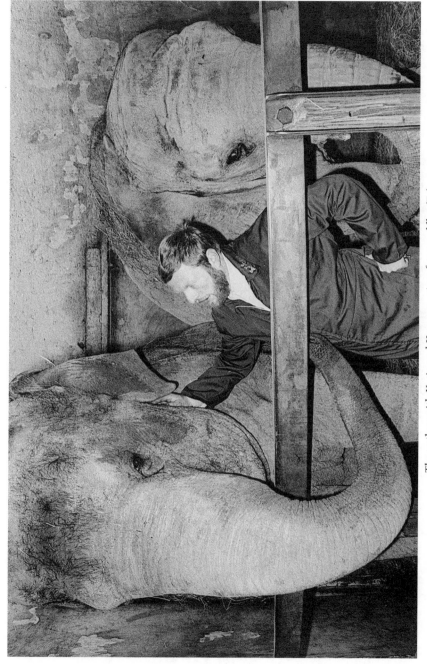

The author with Katie and Kumara - time for a cuddle. (Fr)

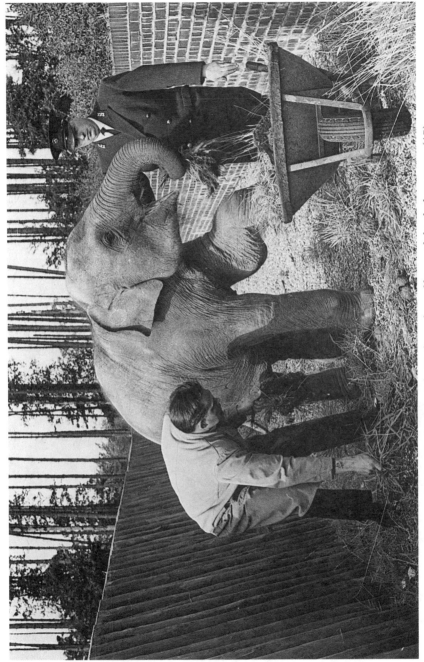

Kumara helping Head Keeper John Datlin and myself to weed the elephant moat. (AP)

44

Another acquisition was shortly to arrive from London Zoo. This was a six-year-old forest bull elephant, by the name of Jumbo! From day one, my worry was whether or not we would be able to contain this animal as he got older. I was informed by the management after making my concerns known that adequate provisions would be made for Jumbo in the near future. The compound would be strengthened and a crush would be provided for handling the elephant. The latter would be essential for attending to foot care and veterinary needs, particularly as this bull would be subject to musth in the years to come. From the day Jumbo arrived there were safety procedures laid down to which all staff would have to adhere. It was apparent this animal was more aggressive than the cows to which we were already accustomed. There would always have to be two people in attendance, as with the cows, and any change in behaviour was logged. Jumbo had the habit of awaiting his opportunity to charge at you if you made the mistake of turning your back on him for a second.

Eventually he began to be bullied by Katie and Kumara - Kumara in particular. She would await any opportunity to either kick him or head butt him! Man and not nature had created this situation - by putting Jumbo in an unnatural environment from where he could not retreat, with bars on one side and a moat on the other! In his normal environment this situation would not have arisen. In the wild, gestures would have been made to him by larger and more dominant bulls, making him submissive in behaviour and therefore he would move out of the way, which was impossible in the compound set-up. So, it was decided that we would separate Jumbo from the cows, for his own safety and ours!

CHAPTER 6
"Care and Treatment of Common Elephant Ailments"

Let us now talk about Asian elephants - their health and build. An elephant is in perfect health when its skin is nearly black and bristly to the touch. The mucous membrane of the mouth and tongue should have a rich pink colour without black spots on the palate. The light spots on the head and trunk should have a natural appearance, as the colour of these spots changes with the health of the elephant. The eye should have a bright, clear appearance and not look contracted at any time of the day. The animal should always be in motion by either swinging the trunk, flapping the ears or moving about. They should take their fodder well and sleep for two to four hours in the night. When awake they should at once commence eating again. The pulsation of the heart should be 49 per minute. Without the greatest care and attention being paid to diet, work and rest, an elephant's health could easily deteriorate.

Amongst some of the general diseases is a fever, where the animal is found to be shivering over the whole body and the trunk becomes cold and contracted. The animal stops feeding, is weak, drowsy and listless and, on occasions, will fall down. Inflammation of the brain is another ailment. This affliction usually commences with a tremulous state of the whole body, extremities and trunk, and the animal makes constant endeavours to free itself. It stretches itself frequently, raises its trunk in the air and tries to strike any person approaching it. Mumps is another disease which could strike the animal. The whole neck becomes swollen, as well as the glands below and behind the ears. Inflammation of the lungs makes the elephant very restless and the animal will not lie down. Its mouth is open wide and frequently it will cough several times in the air as the disease advances. Inflammation of the kidneys makes the animal pass urine by drops at the beginning of the attack. On the same day it becomes totally suppressed, with the abdomen swollen; it is restless and leaves off taking fodder. Diarrhoea is a disorder to which elephants are too often subjected. There are three distinct forms to this disease, namely; indigestion, extreme

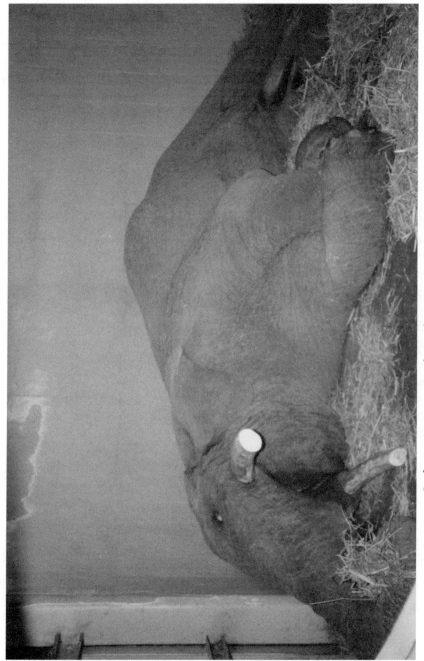

Jumbo in recovery position having been given a reversal drug. (CT)

change in temperature and worms. The latter can be difficult to eradicate without the help of veterinary drugs. Although this infection cannot be considered an illness, the animal requires great care and attention. Some eye problems can occur such as infections and inflammation. These are generally treated by the veterinary officer with antibiotics. It is thought that the tusks of the elephant are not subject to any internal causes. However, they are liable to fracture and, in which case, infections are likely to take hold. On occasions a tusk may have to be partly or completely removed. A horny fungus near the nails, which is likely to run into sores, is more common with working elephants in the wild, and particularly in the wet season. It has been observed in animals in captivity when the feet are constantly wet. Colic is another ailment, which is commons in zoos. The animal leaves off feeding, appears very restless and distressed, one minute lying down, the other rising up; it moves from side to side and opens its mouth frequently. It will cross its legs often and strike its side with "It's tail and will also strike its stomach with its trunk.

To understand fully the diseases and ailments of the elephant one needs to know about the structure of the animal. The word ìelephantî is derived from the Ancient Greek word 'elephas'. The skin of the elephant is from half an inch to one inch thick, loose and, with the aid of a special muscle that lies beneath it, an elephant can make a spasm of movement ripple along the entirety of its body, and so be able to shake off insects and blood-sucking flies. Although the skin is thick, it is also very sensitive to insect bites and flies and so the elephant will constantly throw dust and mud over its body to keep insects at bay. In spite of the thickness of its skin, an African or Asiatic elephant is not equipped with an effective heating mechanism and is therefore confined to areas close to the equator. Body temperature in the morning is about 97° and in the evening about 97.4°F.

The length, at birth, of the trunk is between 10 and 15 inches, but, as the animal grows and the trunk is in constant use, it grows longer, thicker and stronger. The trunk has no bones but many, many muscles and is, in actual fact, its nose, its hands, its everything. Just as the trunk is the elongated nose, the tusks are elongated incisor teeth located in the upper jaw, continuing to grow throughout the elephant's life. Elephants have six sets of front grinding molars throughout this lifetime. The final set begins to appear at 25 - 30 years of age and is usually worn out completely

Foot-care - trimming toenails and cutting off horny fungi. (CT)

Rubbing down dead and flaking skin. (CT)

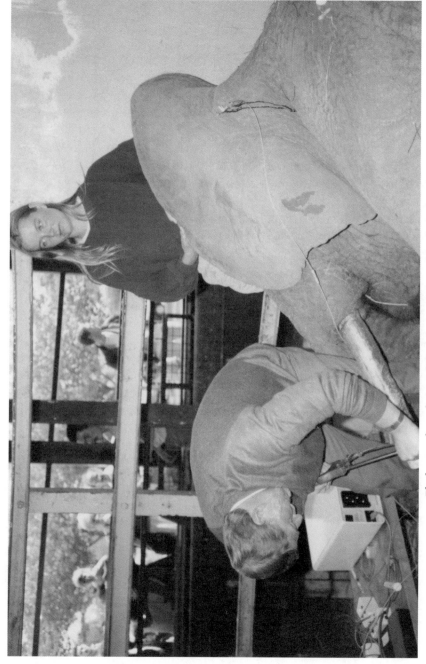

Elephant under sedation while tusks are shortened by the author. (CT)

around 60 years of age, 60 - 70 being the maximum for an elephant's life-span. However, some reading this book will know that there are exceptions to this rule.

The Asiatic tail, at birth, averages 18 inches in length and may grow up to three and a half feet. Some Burmese timber elephants have been recorded at five feet and one inch! In actual fact not many Burmese timber elephants can boast having long tails as they have either been bitten off during fights or eaten away by ulceration, mainly due to disability or old age. A good tuft of bristles at the tip of the tail is as rare as a long tail. The bristles are stiff and hard and about as thick as a toothpick. I have seen them, in the wild, where they have been cut off by mahouts, who make rings and bracelets from them. This also occurs in zoos in the West. An African elephant tail can be as long as five feet on a large animal and has long coarse hairs on the two edges. The tail is used as an indicator of emotion and when the animal is alarmed or frightened, or even angry, the tail is raised in an arc and can be seen in charges or mock play among juveniles. Elephants do not naturally hold each other's tails in the wild or walk in straight lines. The tail holding is a circus-trained spectacle!

Four columns of flesh and muscle support the extraordinary weight, the feet acting like a shock absorber as the animal walks. An average step of an adult in full stride is about five feet over undulating ground. In Burma, some elephants appear more "leggy" than others do and these, as far as timber elephants go, are considered to be of a poorer class than those with short, stumpy ones and are consequently of less value. The elephant has a kind of wrist near the ground, but the elbow is where the leg joins the body. In other words the knee and hock joints are situated very low down. The joints are clearly evident when the animal is in a kneeling position. When an elephant walks, first its heel and then its toes touch the ground. The foot is made up of spongy pads of a fatty substance, which is about one and a half inches thick. It is these spongy pads that act like silencers when the animal walks. This enables the elephant to pull its feet out of muddy holes caused by its own weight. The circumference of the front foot is useful in roughly estimating the height of the animal.

In comparison to the size of the animal, the eyes appear very small. Having poor eyesight, the animal is naturally very cautious. Therefore, it is essential that they have a very keen sense of smell and hearing. Beyond a hundred yards they are unable to distinguish forms but are capable of

Vet inspecting elephant's tail after treatment for an infection. (CT)

noticing movement. He can, however, with ease see objects on either side of his head or in front of him. In order to see objects behind him he is compelled to turn his body either to the left or right. The most common kind of eye is dark brown, but pearly blue eyes are extremely rare. When I was in Thailand we were invited to the Royal Stables where there was a large collection of elephants - some man killers and one sacred white elephant. Two of the elephants which I observed had lovely blue eyes. The eyes have a sliding membrane which the elephant will draw across at the least sign of anyone trying to touch them, as they really positively dislike them being tampered with. As the animal grows older the eyes tend to become more watery and lose the brightness within.

The ears are not just used for flapping and fanning away irritants, but in the African elephant in particular, they act as a cooling device. The back of an African elephant's ear is like a map where the veins can often be seen near to the surface acting as a cooling system. These veins are more difficult to observe on the Asiatic elephant. On the other hand, ears are a good indication of the animal's age. On an elephant of 60 - 70 years of age, the edges of the ears are likely to be torn and tattered and of a lighter colour. The veterinary department would often look for prominent veins in the ear in order to take blood or for giving intravenous injections. Also the mahouts use these areas by applying pressure with their knees or toes to control the animal during training.

Carrying on with the structure of the elephant, nature has given an elephant a short, thick neck which enables it to carry, well above the ground, its massive head which weighs roughly about six per cent of its total body weight. The girth of the neck is almost equal to the height of the elephant's measurement at the shoulder.

To an inexperienced eye it can be difficult to tell the difference between the male, especially the tuskless Asian one, and the female. The female's external organs are not where you would think they should be! The genital opening, or vulva, occupies the position of the penis in the male, and not near the anus as in the case of other quadrupeds. The testicles of the male elephant cannot be observed externally and are completely covered in a sheath. In an adult male elephant the penis, when fully extended, is from two to three feet long, two to three inches in diameter, fleshy and dark purple in colour with a Y-shaped opening at its extremity.

It has been recorded that the gestation period for Asian elephants ranges from 17½ months to 23 months, but for the African it is 22 months. Females are receptive for breeding from 12 years onwards. I will deal, in depth, with the sexual cycle of the cow and the musth of the bull elephant in a later chapter.

CHAPTER 7
"Expedition to East Africa"

As the months passed, I was to read all I could find on elephants and their behaviour. I also spent time just watching or studying them. From this early stage, it was becoming obvious to me that I was studying an animal which is in a totally alien environment and, as I had always thought, their behavioural pattern could not be that of a normal animal living in the wild. If not kept occupied they could so easily develop the stereotyped behaviour I had witnessed in my early days at London Zoo. I considered it extremely important that training sessions on a regular basis were advantageous to trainee keepers and young elephants. This was much to the displeasure of the public on some occasions as, whilst observing the animals during training with their loud, excitable noise and behaviour, they thought it cruel and would complain to the office. It was therefore decided by the management, at my request, that we had information telling the public exactly what we were doing and the reasons behind it. On most occasions, when we explained, the public understood.

One day, David Jones, the Senior Veterinary Officer, mentioned that he was trying to get together a mixed group of twelve people to go "on safari" to Kenya, and wondered if I would be interested. The cost of this venture would be £500, which for 1974 was a considerable amount for me to contemplate spending, let alone saving for! After discussing this with my wife Sheila, it was decided that I would go. Fortunately payments could be made monthly over the next two years for this holiday, But I still needed to undertake odd jobs such as gardening, giving talks, doing painting and decorating and working over-time whenever available at the Zoo.

In my quest for knowledge on these animals in their natural environment, the trip was a most exciting prospect. During the months before we were due to leave, we attended lectures and had discussions on what would be involved and what we could hope to achieve. We were split

One of the beautiful shrubs in the grounds of the Safari Park Hotel, Kenya. (RS)

into four groups of three and allocated our duties for the month. Mine fell under the category of camp security and transport.

Our departure date from the United Kingdom was to be at the beginning of October. We were to leave Heathrow by East African Airways and the journey would last 15 hours, arriving at Nairobi Airport early in the morning. After touchdown we descended from the aircraft and made our way across the tarmac to the arrival hall. The heat was very apparent, which seemed to complement the bright colours worn by the locals. We then travelled by bus to the Safari Park Hotel, just outside Nairobi, where we stayed for a night enjoying the luxury of the swimming pool, the bar and the beautiful fauna in the grounds of the hotel.

The time at the hotel was also spent arranging the pick up of the Volkswagen Combis, which we were to drive ourselves. This was not the 'norm', as they had always previously wanted to give you a driver/guide. The following morning we went to the supermarket for two weeks supply of food, which ranged from various fruits and vegetables to steaks and Tusker lagers! By mid-afternoon of that day we had sorted out the four drivers, with me being one of them plus a co-driver. In the other vehicle were David Jones and his co-driver. We made a conscious decision that we must have at least two people in camp at all times. With the exception of the drivers, the other members of the party would have to take their turn in camp for security reasons.

We headed towards the Masai Mara game reserve, arriving approximately two hours before sunset. We selected a campsite outside the game reserve near a dried up riverbed, under a large tree. We spent the two hours before dusk setting up camp. One party was sent out on wood detail, being advised to keep away from dense areas until we knew what the terrain held and what company we might encounter! The other party pitched the tents and started to prepare dinner.

When my party arrived back at camp with the wood supplies I discovered a horrible mess all over my vehicle! On close examination it proved to be fresh blood. Tracing the source of the blood, I noticed an object wedged in the branches above. Making sure firstly that there were no unwelcome guests in the tree, I climbed up, discovering a male baboon, which had obviously been the kill of a leopard earlier. We decided that Mr Leopard would not return to the kill due to our presence there and that the smell from the dead baboon, thanks to its rotting flesh in the heat of the

Part of a herd seen whilst in the Mara. (RS)

day, would intensify. We decided to remove the carcass from the tree and stake it out about 100 yards from our camp in a clearing, before training the unlit vehicle headlights on the carcass, hoping it would attract scavengers later that night. After our barbecue around our raging log fire we thought we would try our luck by turning on the headlights. To our joy we observed hyena and jackal and also heard the sounds of a lion. Within minutes the carcass had been devoured, so this was an exciting start to our time in the Masai Mara.

The next morning we were awakened by visitors from above, vervet monkeys raiding the fruit and vegetable tent! I arrived there to see one vervet monkey escaping up a tree with one of our oranges. It was obvious that the tent had not been secured and battened down properly to deter these little perishers from scrounging our food.

The next visitors to arrive were a contingent from the Masai village not far away. They showed great interest in these insipid white intruders who had invaded their environment. These Masai tribesmen were to become part of our everyday life in camp, and like the vervet monkeys would often be seen retreating with a bunch of bananas or a few apples.

One young boy, I particularly remember, had pestered me for a few days for an empty green wine bottle. In the end I succumbed and gave him the bottle, which he took down to the dry riverbed and, the sand still being moist, he poured it into the bottle, shaking it to clean it. Having completely cleaned it, it glistened like new. I was wondering constantly what his intentions were. He then walked along the riverbed placing the bottle on a root of a large tree. Returning along the same riverbed, he then picked up stones, which he threw at the bottle until it was smashed! So he was not a lot different from most young boys of his age!

Our nearest port of call for water was Keekorok Lodge, being 15 miles away. It was interesting to see American and German visitors at the Lodge who had flown in for a few days safari. Equipped with dummy ammunition belts across their chest and camouflage jackets, they would prop up the bar with a scotch in their hands, recounting their time in the bush! At the Lodge we filled our large drums with enough drinking water to last us for about four days. The ruling was that if anyone wanted to wash their hair, they would have to do this with water from the river, which had nearly dried up now! This did not go down well with the ladies in our party, as they had to boil the water as well! This was also the rule for bathing and washing.

Young Impala in the Game Lodge, Kenya. (RS)

On one of our excursions out into the bush we noticed two rhinoceros were standing rump to rump, like a pair of bookends. One bright spark in the party asked if I could get closer for him to take some photographs. The terrain was quite undulating and I could see this as a potential problem, unless I could see a way in and an exit path. The vehicle, not being a four-wheel drive, was not robust enough for bouncing about over potholes. Eventually I discovered a track in and an exit. As we approached the rhinos they were not amused at our arrival. Getting the vehicle in a position for quick get-a-way, the lads proceeded to take their photographs. It was not many minutes before the rhinos decided to investigate us further. As they approached at what seemed to be a fast pace I decided it was the time to beat a hasty retreat. My foot coming off the clutch too fast caused the Combi to stall. My thoughts were "Oh shit!" However, I managed to get the vehicle started, just in time for our get-a-way. On our arrival back at camp my passengers related to David about our adventure and he remarked "Well you're back, aren't you?"!

One day, whilst observing the bird life through his binoculars, David suddenly halted his scanning of the bush and said, "Who the hell is that?"Calling me over to where he stood he said "Am I seeing things or is that one of our party in the bush?" Looking through my binoculars I confirmed that it was one of ours with a herd of Cape Buffalo to his right in the thicket and baboons directly ahead of him. Oblivious to this, he continued his bird watching. David's comments were "Where does he think he is - bloody Hyde Park?"

We spent two invaluable weeks here in the beautiful Masai Mara. On returning to Nairobi for provisions the lead vehicle being driven by Sir David encountered mechanical problems. This was to be my chance to take over as lead vehicle, because I had to tow the sod for 90 miles. The rope repeatedly broke, therefore the distance between vehicles gradually became shorter and the dust greater for those in the towed vehicle. We eventually stopped at a small place called Narok. Making enquiries from the local shopkeeper, we discovered that there was a blacksmith whose workshop was on a nearby hillside. Towing the vehicle to the smithy and after asking his advice, he said that he could temporarily fix the vehicle for our return to Nairobi. This work took four hours and after haggling and bartering the price was agreed and our journey continued. Arriving back in Nairobi at 18.00 hours we drove to the vehicle hire centre where

In for a dip. (RS)

Quenching my thirst! (RS)

Small herd crossing the river in search of green pastures. (RS)

immediate attention was given to the vehicle and my Combi required four new tyres.

After replacement of stores we spent a night in the Safari Park Hotel. The following morning we headed off for an appointment with the game warden at Lake Naivasha. On arrival we were invited to his house for drinks on the veranda. He explained to us that because we were so close to a town there were no large carnivores in the park. This was becoming a problem because this meant that there were no predators to keep the game down. There was a suggestion that leopards should be re-introduced into the area, as the baboons were becoming a problem. After our drinks and lunch we were escorted to the lake which had a shimmering haze of pink over it. We were told that there were an estimated quarter of a million flamingos feeding in the lake.

We left Lake Naivasha, heading for Maru National Park, approximately 150 miles away. Following David at about quarter of a mile apart, due to the flying dust, we entered a small village. As I approached their vehicle I realised there was a problem. Apparently they had hit a pick up truck full of workmen on their way home. The truck had signalled to turn left and then the driver changed his mind and turned right into the path of the on coming Combi that was driven by David Jones' co-driver Richard, who was most distraught.

It happened to be Kenyatta day, a national holiday, which meant that there was no police presence in the surrounding area. Under David's instructions, I was asked to take statements and draw a plan of the area and the accident. It turned out that when the workmen's pick up was struck, they were thrown from the vehicle and one of them had sustained a broken arm. In a matter of minutes, irate Africans surrounded the whole area. After much discussion we proceeded to the police station. On our arrival we found they were all "Brahms and Liszt!" The senior officer suggested we should return at noon the next day.

We continued our journey to Maru National Park. On our arrival we met the game warden, an ex-army Englishman, who showed us our banda, a straw-roofed hut, in which we would sleep for the next week. That evening during the barbecue Richard became very agitated and worried about what would befall him in connection with the accident. So I spent most of the evening reassuring the poor chap that he would not be interned! The next morning David, Richard and myself returned to the

Village in the Maru National Park. (RS)

scene of the accident, where we were met by a senior police officer who told us we would meet the driver of the pick-up truck involved in the accident. Having waited for over an hour it was apparent that he was not going to turn up. The police officer suggested that we should all drive to Maru police station some miles away. Arriving at the headquarters, we alighted from the vehicle, expecting him to escort us inside the building. This was not the case! It turned out that Chappie, our policeman, only wanted a lift! When he was asked about the incident he said "You can go, leave it to me!"

Once again we drove back to Maru National Park. As we approached camp, Alan, my co-driver, came running towards us. David, stopping, wound down his window, saying, "What's the problem?" Alan replied "I've 'ad an accident Mr Jones." I said, "What sort of an accident?" He replied "I've 'it anuvver car." I said, "You haven't damaged my car have you, you little shit?" He said "No, but the uvver one's a bit of a mess!" It turned out he was on the brow of a small incline, watching game, unaware of a following vehicle. Obviously failing to look in his mirror, he released the hand brake, rolling backwards, caving in a German gentleman's car, doing substantial damage to the engine. The German had already obtained a statement from Alan admitting full responsibility, which I tore up, much to the German's annoyance, telling him he would have to deal directly with his and our insurers.

Our stay in Mairu National Park was to be one of great interest, with herds of game to observe. It was usual to see gerenuk antelope standing on their hind legs feeding from tall shrubs and herds of impala and Grant's gazelle feeding on open savannah. We also managed to see black rhinoceros, white rhinoceros and lots of Cape buffalo, common Duiker, water buck, bush buck and last but not least Hartebeest or Kangoni and on rare occasions, elephants.

Whilst on the subject of elephants, there was an incident which occurred at about 02.00 am, when I knocked on the door of Alan and Shirley, to ask him if he would come and take a picture of a large bull elephant that had wandered into camp. Opening the door, bleary-eyed, after some discussion he agreed and got dressed! We quietly and stealthily approached our quarry, keeping downwind, so as not to alert this magnificent beast, feeding quietly in the slightly chilled moonlight air. This exercise proved to be a great success for we obtained numerous shots

Large bull elephant that wandered into our camp one evening. (RS)

Too close fro comfort! (RS)

with our friend unaware of our presence. On returning to Alan's banda, I sat on his porch, smoking a cigarette, as he entered his abode. I could hear voices from inside. Shirley was enquiring as to what I had wanted of him. After Alan explained what we had been up to, there was a pause in the conversation and she then replied. "Do you mean to say that he got you up in the middle of the night to take a picture of a bloody elephant - wait until I see him in the morning!" Needless to say, dawn approached, with a magnificent ball of fire rising above the horizon. As I sat drinking my coffee Shirley appeared with non-stop verbal complaints regarding my early morning photography caper, which she religiously recounted to all of our party.

The drive to Adamsons' falls, named after George and Joy Adamson, proved very interesting, with viewing of Crocodile, Warthog, Hyena, Vervet monkeys, Olive baboon and Mongoose. We also had sighting of very varied bird life such as Grey Hornbill, Drongo, European Roller, Kori Bustard, Marabou Stork, Pale Chanting Goshawk, Paradise Flycatcher, Pied Kingfisher, Pigmy Falcon and Tawny Eagle.

Unfortunately, one of our party, Geoff, a senior keeper from London Zoo, had been diagnosed at Nanyuki Hospital with hepatitis and was required to remain there until we were ready to leave Kenya for the U.K, consequently missing all the experiences of the National Park. We had all been inoculated before our travels, including hepatitis A and B, so this was so unfortunate that he still contracted the disease. He, however, made a full recovery on returning to England.

Many times, whilst touring around, we would meet Europeans who were farmers, game wardens or just Kenya residents. Consequently we had many invitations for dinner. On one of these, the younger members of the party were asked to partake in a little exercise! Having no idea what form this would take, we all clambered into the back of an open Landrover. As we drove through the darkness we came upon a hyena eating one of our host's sheep. On our arrival at the carcass, the hyena took flight. The farmer concluded that the sheep had died of natural causes and had not fallen foul to the hyena. We continued on with increasing speed and one of us was asked to turn the spotlight on and scan the area for Spring Hares. The idea was that we should get as close as possible before jumping from the vehicle, in full flight, endeavouring to catch one of the most agile and nimble creatures. As we covered this uneven surface, I stumbled, finding

Author having a siesta or was it due to the alcohol! (RS)

myself completely winded, rear-end jammed in what turned out to be a wart-hog hole, much to the amusement and laughter of the entire party. Eventually they retrieved me from my temporary accommodation. Regaining my breath and composure and dusting myself down, I clambered into the pick-up truck. My exciting expedition for the night had come to an abrupt end! This was much discussed over large scotches back at the ranch!

Sadly to say, our trip to Kenya was now coming to a close. We had one more night to spend in The Safari Park Hotel, just outside Nairobi. The month since our arrival had just flown by, as the next morning we had to board our flight back to Heathrow and our drive back to Whipsnade.

CHAPTER 8
"Back in the Wilds of Bedfordshire"

We had a couple of days to reflect and unwind before our return to work. Arriving at the elephant house at 07.00 hrs, there was a noisy reception which brought the Park Manager, Mr Chamberlain, into his rear garden overlooking the compound. Seeing it was me he just waved, and retired inside for his breakfast. At 08.00 hrs the rest of the staff arrived to bring me up to date with what had happened in the last month.

First on the agenda was the marked deterioration in Jumbo's behavioural pattern. This animal was now approximately 11 years old and requiring three keepers to stable him every night. One keeper had to observe from the passage, one to close the door and one to watch the elephant's movements while the door was being closed and locked in position. This procedure had to be followed rigorously, as Jumbo had been known, on many occasions, to turn on a penny and pursue the keeper who was trying to lock the stable door.

Discussions were now beginning about the departure of Metdere, the 7-foot African elephant, to Edinburgh Zoological Gardens on permanent loan. We were to receive an elephant travelling crate a week before departure to Edinburgh so that the animal would get used to going in and out of it. Due to normal delays, the crate arrived only two days before departure, so I decided that we would feed Metdere morning and evening in the crate. First day, no joy. Metdere flatly refused to enter. By the evening of the second day, her stomach getting the better of her, she decided to enter for the food.

The following morning a low-loader arrived from an Aylesbury transport company. The load consisted of an elephant, a rhinoceros and some deer. We had an early start, with a route mapped out to encounter very few roundabouts. Our driver was a patient man, of vast experience with such heavy loads. We started off on the M1 with much amusement to other road users who would see, periodically, a trunk appearing through the top of the crate. Even funnier, when we stopped for refreshment in the transport areas near trees, was the sight of the trunk reaching for branches and on one occasion dismembering a large branch from an oak tree!

On arrival at Edinburgh Zoo, it was apparent that a large crane was needed to swing the elephant in the crate, over the moat, into the outside compound. The crate was placed in such a position, so that theoretically the animal would walk from the crate to its inside enclosure. Having positioned the crate and with the crane having been moved away, I was to discover that the crate was round the wrong way. This meant that I would have to open the crate at the rear end, crawl between Metdere's legs to her head and reverse her out! I was only prepared to do this if, firstly, the house was cleared of public, zoo officials and pressmen. The first reaction was that this could not be done, as they all wanted to view the unloading. After I had pointed out the dangers to myself if the animal became startled, the house was then cleared. Apprehensively I crawled to the front of the crate, reassuring Metdere constantly. To everyone's relief this all went as planned and the elephant reversed into her new abode.

On my return from Edinburgh Zoo I learnt that I was now also to take charge of the Dolphinarium. This being a recent addition to the park, I found there was a certain atmosphere towards me during my daily visits. The keeper in situ resented any comments from the Head Keeper of the elephant section. However, this was duly rectified by discussions over the training of the dolphins.

It took considerable time for me to understand the complete workings of the filtration plant as the water was chlorinated to four parts per million, to ward off any fungal or bacterial infections which could be harmful to the dolphins. The salt content or pH was kept at about 7.8 and the chlorine level was kept between 3 and 1 or 4 and 1. This was checked two to three times a day with instruments.

There were occasions when the dolphins had to be removed from the pool, for example, due to sickness, or the need to be weighed or for transport to other zoos. On all of these occasions the presence of the veterinary officer was essential. The removal of some one hundred pounds of dolphin was not always an easy task. Firstly, the mammal would be isolated into a smaller area and with two or three keepers in the water it was manoeuvred to a shallow shelf, the idea being to manhandle the

Staff being presented to Princess Margaret on the occasion of the opening of the dolphinarium. (LZ)

Warm-up session. (LZ)

The power of the dolphin to project its body high out of the water is clearly demonstrated. (LZ)

Dolphins being trained to jump out of water and through a hoop. (LZ)

Balls being retrieved and presented to the trainer. (LZ)

dolphin into a sling before lifting it onto the side of the pool. This did not always go to plan, as the dolphin would resist by slashing its tail in the water, with keepers flying in different directions. We certainly needed the aqua-lung training in all aspects of the job, as given by the Bedfordshire Police Diving Section. With perseverance, we finally succeeded in raising the dolphin from the pool and t was then essential to keep the dolphin constantly wet to avoid the skin drying out.

After a year I relinquished my duties at the dolphinarium to concentrate on pachyderms. However, this could not be exclusively so, because my section now comprised Congo buffalo, musk oxen, squirrel monkeys, sea lions, vultures and a paddock of roan antelope and water buck. I already had the chimp house next door to the elephants and I was also expected to train staff in the handling of the latter. This proved to be very difficult due to the fact that Katie and Kumara were now increasing in size and devilment, taking advantage when my second-in-command or myself were not around.

This strain continued to be the case for a number of years until 1980. Then I was speaking to a young lady in the Children's Zoo who showed a lot of interest in elephants. Making enquiries of my superiors I learnt that she was a temporary summer hostess in the Children's Zoo by the name of Carla and that she had worked with large horses and was an accomplished rider. I asked my bosses if she could be transferred to my section and their initial reaction was negative, fearing that she would not be any good with elephants. I suggested that they should let me be the judge of that. After some weeks they allowed her to work with me for a trial period. It was obvious from the first day that her interest was like a breath of fresh air; she asked questions constantly and showed a genuine fascination with these large beasts and more importantly, when accompanying me into the stables, she did as I suggested and remembered all I had told her on how to conduct herself in their presence.

CHAPTER 9
"Off to the Desert!"

In 1983 a meeting was held in the Main Office with David Jones to discuss the setting up of a Zoo, to be designed by J. S. Bonningtons of St. Albans, in Qatar in the United Emirates which required a supply of senior keepers, a veterinary officer and a manager to head the project. The Zoological Society of London would have to source over 2,000 animals to stock this Zoo in Qatar. This also included all the animals' food, initially for a year.

After listening to David Jones for about an hour and a half I asked him if I would be wasting my time in applying for the second-in-charge position. He said that he did not think that I would be interested as I was a married man, but the job was mine if I wanted it. I said that I would go home and discuss it with my wife, Sheila, as this job would involve being away overseas for one year. Her reaction was that it would be a wonderful experience and challenge and after considerable thought I told David I would like to accept his offer.

The talks that followed with David meant that we would be advertising within The Zoological Society of London and elsewhere for experienced keepers in their fields: - large carnivores, hoof stock, birds, insects, reptiles and small mammals. After much discussion the team selected was Fred Smith, an excellent bird-keeper; Frank Wheeler, an experienced small-mammal man; Paul Anscombe, who had spent many years in the lion house in London Zoo; Terry Hornsey, a very young, but very good hoof-stock keeper and last, but not least, Frank Leftwich to cover insects and reptiles, known by the nickname "praying mantis." David Jones also invited me up to London to meet Dr. Tom Begg whom he had appointed as Manager for the Doha project. Tom, a very dapper gentleman, was a qualified veterinary surgeon with a vast experience. He had spent 10 years in Jersey Zoo working with Gerald Durrell and subsequently John Aspinall at Howletts and Port Lympne. He was to be seconded for two years to the Doha project.

My wife Sheila, son Martin, David Jones and myself left Heathrow at the beginning of June 1983 for Qatar in the Persian Gulf, arriving 10 days before the main shipment of animals. At Doha airport we immediately became aware of the extreme heat and the presence of armed Police. Happily we were met by the secretary of the architects' department who drove us to The Ramada Hotel in the centre of Doha.

The following morning we made an early start and the first job on the agenda was to acquire a vehicle for getting to work, as the Zoo was eight miles from Doha. Unfortunately the car was not wholly suitable, as it had no air conditioning.

Arriving at the Zoo, we were met by Dr. Pharmi, an Egyptian vet who had, until recently, been in charge, so it was a case of being extremely diplomatic as I would be working alongside him over the months ahead. With the assistance of Dr. Pharmi, my first priority was to check all menagerie enclosures, cages, aviaries, all safety devices, locks and bolts, for the safety of keepers, public and animal collections. I found many defects, particularly in the lion house. Wire mesh on outside enclosures was of insufficient height; the leopards' outside enclosures had to be covered in; gaps between locking bolts on dividing cages in the service areas had to be made smaller and there was inadequate viewing in the den area. These, with many other alterations, had to be carried out immediately, as we were expecting the large shipment within 10 days.

In 2 to 3 days I submitted my list to the architects' department, with a photocopy to the municipality, the governing body of the Zoo. Promptly, I was asked by the Arabs to condense the list to priority jobs only, which I said I had done by submitting only 120 jobs instead of the original 200! The outside contractors and our works department carried out these tasks very efficiently and promptly.

I was informed that on the following Monday morning I had to report to immigration to start the paperwork for my resident's permit. I was to see bureaucracy at its worst! Luckily Sheila accompanied me on these occasions, which proved to be invaluable, as the Arabs did not like to keep women waiting! Even so, this process took a long time over the following weeks.

One of the jobs Sheila had come to do was to equip all the keeping staff from London, including myself, with furniture and kitchen appliances. Sometimes she was accompanied by David Jones to do this mammoth task.

The keepers had their own individual sleeping quarters with a shared kitchen and lounge and I had a flat in the Sheikh's Palace, which was also in the Zoo grounds. All my staff's accommodation, including my own, was air-conditioned and had hot and cold running water.

I was told by David Jones that Tom Begg, the vet, who was to be the Project Manager, would arrive in approximately 3 months time - after the initial setting-up of the Zoo - this meant that the preliminary work would be down to us, including the training of many nationalities of young and old keepers in the care and management of animals, many lectures, with interpreters and of course, on-site training with our own London Zoo staff. My job was to oversee that training.

Ibraham, a Somali gentleman, was appointed as Stores Keeper and with my help, organised a system for checking all food in and out of the area, including a written record. Other appointments at the Zoo were Mike Kock, a vet from America, the brother of the vet at Whipsnade Zoo; Dr. Nabil, an Egyptian vet and Dr. Abdi, a Somali vet. These were to be trained in different wild animal techniques by Dr. Kock and, of course, Dr. Begg. Sadly, over dinner one night Dr. Pharmi informed Sheila, myself and David that he was returning to the slaughter house - in fact, his previous job.

My flat, in the Sheikh's palace, was now furnished and ready for me to move in. It was on the third floor, with a beautiful marble staircase leading up to the veranda and entrance to the flat, which overlooked the zoo grounds with their beautiful fauna and flora and water gardens. The whole of the zoo garden area had underground irrigation, with desalinated water from the sea.

It was now nearing the time for the departure of livestock from Heathrow, with BBC TV coverage. I think that at my end we were as ready as we could be to receive this large shipment, except for last minute checks, which proved to be satisfactory. Eventually, early one morning I was informed that the shipment had arrived at Doha airport and would be arriving in the zoo grounds within two to two and a half hours.

After a briefing from David, we all proceeded to uncrate our charges. One man in particular who was invaluable was Ian Gibb, an animal dealer from Bedfordshire who had accompanied the shipment. He had first class knowledge of the crating up of the animals, for example the way in which they were facing, as it was not always possible to see through the hessian on some of the crates. And last but by no means least - his tool kit! By late evening unloading was complete.

Ibraham, Somali Stores Keeper. (JF)

The following morning I walked the gardens with David. The first thing we discovered was the male wallabies up to their necks in the water troughs, cooling off. It was ironic; they had left snow in England and arrived in this extreme heat. In the initial settling-in period we only lost one young Nilgai from heat stroke. As we continued our walk around the zoo, we checked on all our new arrivals and chatted to the keepers from India to Somalia to Jordan and to Egypt. They were delighted with their new charges, which seemed to have settled in remarkably well. As we approached the lion house, there was some discussion going on as to the whereabouts of one of the leopards, which could not be seen in the den. So one volunteer was pushed into the den inside a steel crush crate. He immediately informed us that all was well and we still had two leopards! The volunteer was then pulled out in the crate, none the worse for his excitement!

In two weeks time David would return to England and, as Tom Begg was not going to arrive for several months, I was going to be in sole charge until then, reporting to the municipality on the training of the keepers and the day to day running of the zoo gardens. However, Mike Kock, the vet from America, was to arrive shortly and take up his post in the animal hospital as veterinary officer in charge of training, under the supervision of Dr Begg on his arrival.

Having now passed my driving test, which took a whole day (a lot of the time was taken up by standing around waiting for the powers that be to get through the bureaucracy), I was in a position to purchase the Range Rover which had been agreed by David Jones for my own use and senior Zoological Society of London staff - I was also given a GMC pick up truck by the municipality for zoo work, for which I needed a Ministry of Transport Licence! So another driving test had to be taken. Completion of driving tests and immigration documentation took about six weeks!

The next couple of months ran very smoothly, but I had noticed feelings of anxiety and concern, amongst some of the younger Zoological Society of London staff, about their wives and loved ones back home. So I thought it would be a good idea to have a dinner party which would of course include all the keepers - 21 in all. This took place on the lawn in front of the keepers' accommodation but we had to bear in mind the religious beliefs of the Muslim law regarding alcohol. So it was Pepsi and Seven-Up all round! The party went down very well with all concerned,

*A view from the Sheikh's Palace at Doha Zoo -
author with his wife Sheila and son Martin. (JF)*

My Range Rover has just arrived! (JF)

with contributions of food from the Indian keepers, the Egyptian vet and of course the Europeans. The party continued into the early hours and seemed to have the desired effect of raising morale, until I informed them that it would be a normal 06.00 hrs start the next day!

After a period of roughly three months we had weeded out the dead wood and established compatible working groups for the various sections. The training was to be ongoing by Zoological Society of London staff, followed by lectures twice weekly by myself, starting with basic animal husbandry. This included instruction on the cleaning of dens, stables and paddock areas, the cleaning of water troughs and the fundamental welfare

Senior staff of Doha Zoo together with "conscripts" from London Zoo. (JF)

and care of the animals. Every lecture given to the non-European staff required an interpreter, which made the job much harder and longer. In some cases there were different Indian dialects to overcome, but we succeeded in the end!

Yusef -Second in charge of cleaning up in the elephant enclosure. (JF)

I deliberated with David Jones, on one of his visits, about an incentive scheme with a diploma for outstanding achievement over the next twelve months by the new staff. The assessment would have to be of a practical nature due to the language problem. This would include their ability to carry out basic animal husbandry, boxing up animals for departure, public relations, pride in their appearance and of course punctuality. After being given permission from the Municipality and the Zoological Society of London, I told the keepers that the most outstanding amongst them would receive a Zoological Society of London diploma and a book about the animals in their care.

In due course Dr Begg arrived. He was a dapper, 5ft 7ins man, with fair hair and complexion and of slight build. He was immaculately dressed in a conventional navy blazer and grey flannels. My first and last "contre temps" with him happened within 24 hours of his arrival. I was supervising the unloading of stores when a messenger came with a piece of paper in his hand. Reading the note from Tom, it stated that we had one heron loose and one vervet monkey on the outside of its cage and I was required to meet Tom in the animal hospital where he was instructing the vets. Arriving at the entrance door I asked, "Is this message from you?" He replied in the affirmative. I screwed up the piece of paper and threw it in his direction, which unfortunately caught him on the nose! I said that first of all the heron was a wild one, which arrives every morning, and secondly the monkey was a young vervet, which was bred in the aviary and was able to go back and forth through the four-inch mesh due to its size. There was no reply from Tom, so I left and continued with my workload.

It was around eight p.m., just as I had nestled down in an armchair with a book, when there was a knock on my front door. On opening the door, dangling in front of my eyes was an outstretched arm with a bottle of Famous Grouse at the end of it. A voice said "Truce!" My answer was "Enter!" I fetched two tumblers and we consumed the whole bottle of whisky, drinking and talking into the early hours.

Next day after my morning rounds, with a slight hangover and feeling as though an express train had hit me, I arrived at Tom's office. I am pleased to report that he looked and apparently felt as bad as me! We both vowed never to imbibe to that extent again! What a load of rubbish that was!

Tom began to talk about the hands-on management of the park. Drawing a circle, which represented the zoo, he made a large cross, which filled the circle. He said "All that is yours - the keepers, the animals and all the problems that go with it. I will do the office side and deal with the politics of the Municipality and I am available any time you have anything with which you feel you cannot deal. Obviously we will see each other socially on a regular basis over the next twelve months."

Tom's initial stay in Qatar was to be comparatively short-lived. He arrived at my flat to say that he was returning to the United Kingdom forthwith, because he had misunderstandings regarding his position and his office area. He left within twenty-four hours, informing me that I was back in charge once again. He could not give me a date for his return. In fact he was absent for about a month, arriving back accompanied by David Jones, the problems apparently having been resolved.

The following morning, while David, Tom and myself were on our rounds in the gardens, the head keeper of the elephants approached us, with his magnificent five tonne bull elephant in tow! The animal appeared to be rather agitated and I commented to Nyheme that I thought that by his behaviour he might be due to come into musth. His reaction was "No boss, no boss, no musth, no musth." It turned out that he was on his routine walkabout of the grounds. I was not convinced that he was not due to come into musth, so I ordered him to return Moti to the elephant compound immediately. This he did without any argument at all. Thinking this was the end of the problem we proceeded on our rounds.

It was not until eight thirty the next morning that Nyheme came into my office saying "Big problem Mr John, Moti in pond, very aggressive. Refuses to answer to commands. You experienced elephant man from London Zoo, come and sort him out." My reaction was "Oh shit!"

Accompanying Nyheme to the elephant enclosure, I was confronted by five tonne, ten foot at the shoulder, of angry elephant! The first problem was to get Moti out of the pond and to get Tom Begg ready with his immobilising rifle. As soon as I entered the compound, Moti left the pond like a train, heading for all five foot five inches of me! As I sprinted away I could sense the bull gaining on me, my pants getting wetter by the second! Thinking, as I went under the steel arm with a five hundred weight counter balance, that I was safe, the bull however hit the bar with his trunk, sending the whole contraption into slight orbit. I remember, to

Decorated bull elephant - this chalk decoration was a daily ritual with the Indian staff. (JF)

this day, going through the door to my left, flattening the Indian vet in my path who had been watching the whole exercise, and shouting, "Close the door!" This he did, in vain, as Moti put a tusk through the door! Luckily for us the door was of a standard size restricting Moti's advance.

Moti then returned to the compound, where he took his anger out on Camelot, the female Asian elephant. The bull now had to be lured into position for darting. This procedure was to take four hours, as Moti continued to position himself as far away from the musth chains as possible. Eventually, with one long rope with a noose in one end, Moti was coaxed towards the musth chains. Putting one front foot in the noose, the rope was immediately pulled tight, restricting his movement. This was achieved by twenty men on the other end of the rope, which had been threaded through the musth chain ring. The immediate reaction of the bull was to twist the rope in his trunk, making it a "tug-o-war" situation between himself and the twenty men!

It seemed like minutes, but was only seconds before Tom got off a shot into the animal, immobilising him. There was applause all round and from above, where David Jones was showing around the officials from the Municipality. I had been totally unaware of my audience. After close examination, I decided that the bull was in his first stages of musth. This fitted in with his behaviour earlier, with his indifference to his master's words of command and with the swelling of his temples.

THE PHENOMENON OF MUSTH

The manifestation of musth is a natural phenomenon, which a male goes through annually after he has attained the age of maturity. Some say it is comparable to rut, or heat, or a period of sexual desire in other animals. The musth period can be split into four stages.

In the initial stage the animal becomes listless and he has a loss of appetite and refuses to act on commands. The sheath that covers the testicles is descended and the temples swell considerably.

In the second stage the sheath and the temples appear more enlarged and a thick oily substance begins to exude from the temporal glands or musth holes. These are tiny slits, which are located between the eye and the ear on either side of the head. His penis is erect most of the time and occasionally it will jerk up spasmodically and touch his stomach. From appearance the animal is listless but at the slightest sound his ears would spread out, his eyes alert, his body still and tense, and only his trunk would lift up to test the wind.

In the third stage, liquid substance flows not only from the musth holes, but a whitish discharge drips from his penis as well. By now, the penis is fully extended and dangles between his hind legs, nearly touching the ground. At this stage with the lower and upper musth in evidence, the animal is said to be in full musth.

In the fourth and final stage, the oily substance from the musth holes flows almost continuously into the mouth. This is known, by the Burmese, as the musth drinking stage.

MUSTH CHAINS

These are longer and stronger than ordinary chains. They are made of $5/8$ inch chain and up to forty feet long, compared to the ordinary ones of $3/8$ inch chain, and up to thirty feet long. Due to the fact that bulls in musth can be most destructive and dangerous to approach, I had previously sunk a water trough below ground level and the feed pipe to it was three foot below the surface.

Also required were fifteen-foot rakes for the safe removal of dung during this period of musth.

It was in the early hours of one morning some time later when I was suddenly awoken by a loud bang on my door. Having aroused myself, I opened the door to be met by the night watchman. Although his English was poor, I could make out that there was some trouble at the elephant house. I told him that I would meet him there in five minutes.

On my arrival at the compound I could hear quite a commotion going on. As I turned the corner I could make out two figures and another one being that of Moti in the darkness of the early morning. On my approaching and saying, "Who's there?" Nyheme and his brother Yusef came towards me, carrying in each of their hands large poles with spikes on the end. Examining them to the best of my ability in the moonlight, I discovered what I thought to be bloodstains on the metal points. I informed both men that I was confiscating these poles and that I would be back at first light to investigate what had been going on.

At 06.30 hrs Tom Begg and I walked around to the elephant house. Nyheme had apparently covered Moti with sand, obviously to disguise what had happened during the night. I picked up the hosepipe and started to wash the elephant down. As the sand washed off, it became apparent, as I had suspected, that the animal had large areas of punctured flesh, with blood stained wounds.

Having ascertained the reasons for their behaviour, with the help of Dr. Nabil one of the zoo vets, it appeared that this method of spiking the animal was the one used to keep the animal awake, in order, as the Indians thought, to hasten the end of the musth. However, I could not tolerate this treatment of the bull, as it was clearly cruel and barbaric. Due to this incident, Tom and I decided that Moti would have to be sedated for closer examination. Some of the wounds we found were quite deep and one in particular looked as if it may have damaged a bone in the elephant's leg. Moti was cleaned up and given a multi-antibiotics injection and kept under close observation by Mike Kock, the resident vet. It was noticed at a later date, after the subsidence of the musth, that Moti tended to favour the damaged leg when trying to mount Camelot. This wound I suspected was due to the treatment received from the keepers that early morning. With the termination of musth, Moti now responded to commands given by his master Nyheme. This was quite a sight to see. As I walked past in the mornings the elephant was instructed to salute, bow and raise his front right leg as a greeting to me.

One felt very safe whilst in the present of Nyheme such that my son Martin and wife Sheila were able to sit on Moti, but this is not something one would contemplate on one's own. As time passed, Nyheme and I became great friends, exchanging knowledge and experience gained with pachyderms. He was a family man with 12 children and relatives to support back home in India, and was over generous whenever he saw Sheila or Martin, giving silk to Sheila and money to Martin. He was impossible to go shopping with, as he bought anything one looked at - which I found extremely embarrassing.

I told Nyheme that he was to house white rhinos in part of the elephant house, and, unlike his elephants, he would have to be wary of them! However, within weeks of the arrival of the rhinos he was decorating them with chalk and sitting on them, as he had done for years with the elephants, oblivious to any danger!

In the same shipment as the rhinos, came four crocodiles. I asked Tom Begg what he knew about crocodiles. His reply was "Nought." He went on to say that he knew I was a capable man and that I would manage. Smiling, he said that he would return to his office duties and that he would meet me for a drink after the unloading.

The first crate was lowered into the enclosure and apprehensively I

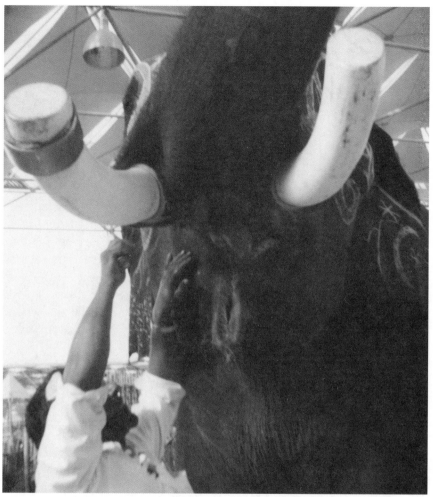

Nyheme instructs the bull elephant to open his mouth for teeth inspection. (JF)

lifted the slide to find that the three-foot crocodile was a six foot one! So, taking hold of its tail, I gave it a large pull, swinging it around into the water, and thinking, one down three to go. As I looked up I saw the smiling faces of the Zoological Society of London staff and the Indian keepers. I said to one of the Zoological Society of London staff "I don't know what you're smiling about, because you can release the next one!" Joining me in the enclosure, I stood back, while he followed my procedure. His crocodile was very alert, swinging around and catching the top of his boot with its teeth, before entering the water. One can imagine how this story grew in the months to come.

The remaining two crocodiles came out comparatively easily. A job well done, considering none of us had handled crocodiles before. This was not to be the end, as Tom informed me two days later that the pond was leaking and that my skills would be needed in recapturing our friends for relocation in the hospital area. With a large grin on his face he said that the crocodiles would be more active as they would have warmed up since their arrival at the zoo!

Mike Kock came up with the idea that he would sedate them. This proved to be non-effective, so we resorted to dog-capture poles, which are telescopic aluminium poles with a rope noose. On his first attempt the crocodile snapped at the pole, biting it in half! With the next attempt we managed to clear the head over the front legs and then dragged the animal into a large crate. There was some difficulty in retrieving the noose, as it had to come over the back legs and tail. For the second crocodile, we overpowered the animal and tied its mouth up. This made the whole procedure much easier and we soon had all four crocodiles in their temporary quarters.

Mike Kock continued to be busy. On one occasion the Barbary sheep had been re-located into the zebra and antelope compound, due to the fact that they had been jumping the moat, out of the paddock they were in. One morning we noticed the male Barbary sheep was failing to put weight onto his front legs. After entering the paddock and examining the animal, Mike took it to the hospital unit for closer examination and informed me later that both front legs were broken. This was probably due to a kick from a zebra stallion. Much to my amazement he decided to plaster the animal's front legs. In the weeks to come it made a full recovery.

The job was proving to be as tough as I thought it might be, having to keep everybody's morale up, with no one to boost my own. With little or no time off initially, I grabbed a few hours here and there to go bird watching at the effluent dump where one could observe flamingos, bee-eaters and ibis.

Occasionally I drove across the desert for 25 miles to reach the coast for a swim. The roads left a lot to be desired and would collapse under the heat of the sun. On one of my many drives, I noticed pieces of rubber

A common sight on my drives across the desert - a Dromedary Camel. (JF)

appearing in front of my windscreen. Unaware that I had driven over anything I stopped to have a look, discovering that I had a puncture on the front wheel. Going around the rear of the vehicle to get the jack I discovered it was incomplete. With the sun scorching down and having broken my own rule about always carrying water in the vehicle, I had a problem! With little or no traffic on this isolated road, I began to turn the jack with a nail I found in the back of the Range Rover. As one could imagine this took some considerable time to get the vehicle jacked up enough to get the wheel off, only to discover that the spare was fully inflated and therefore I had to jack up higher still!

I was now beginning to get rather dry and maybe a little dehydrated when I suddenly thought "Washer bottle!" Opening the bonnet, to my delight the washer bottle was full and for once I had not topped it up with fairy liquid. Removing the hose I siphoned off some water to drink, which tasted very good, although somewhat warm! Mission completed, I continued on for my swim.

On my return to the zoo some worried looking staff wondered what had happened to me, as I had been away for much longer than I had said I would be. Having told them the story, one cheeky sod said, "I thought I might be in for promotion if you hadn't returned!" He then said "No such luck!" I never did discover who had left the jack handle out of the vehicle, but two days later it mysteriously re-appeared back in the boot of the Range Rover!

Everything in the zoo was going as planned and some new staff from London Zoo had arrived. One keeper, Paul Anscombe, was to be our large carnivore man and my number two. I was due to return to the United Kingdom for Christmas for a week's break. I had to set in motion the procedures for leaving the country and obtain an exit visa for myself and members of the United Kingdom staff. On examining their passports I discovered that one had visited Israel. This had obviously been overlooked on his entry into the country, but I could not be sure that it would go unnoticed and not cause problems on his departure. So we notified the British Embassy that our old friend Moti had eaten it. I was not convinced that the Embassy believed our story, but they obliged by supplying a replacement passport.

We were going to depart on the midnight flight from Doha airport to Heathrow, which took seven hours. My wife Sheila and son Martin met me and then we drove home to Whipsnade. Early the next morning I was anxious to go to the zoo to see my elephants. It was a lovely morning for the time of year and the elephants were out in the compound; as I crossed the road Kumara's back was facing me. My only words to her were "How are you, you old bag?" She spun round on a penny and trumpeted and roared in delight. She must have been heard all around the zoo! As I walked round to the keepers' mess room, some staff were working in the stables, others in the food area. The first person I spoke to was Carla, who said "Judging by Kumara's reactions we knew you must be back!" Stepping over the barrier, into the small yard, I called Kumara who was already on her way down the paddock. As she approached the gate it was apparent that she was not going to wait for it to be opened! There was three tonnes of elephant, nine foot at the shoulder, that hit the gate and demolished it! Carla's remarks were "Another works ticket, you will be popular!" Immediately following Katie the elephant's greeting was quite emotional - trumpeting, squeaking, passing urine and dung. I was literally "In the shit!"

After being reunited with my elephants I was updated about the last eight months on the section. Sadly, the behaviour pattern of Jumbo, the forest bull elephant, had deteriorated further. Having become very aggressive, without the proper facilities to contain such an animal, his future at the zoo did not look promising.

At the end of my week's leave, while I was waiting in the departure lounge I was approached by a very large African gentleman who asked if he could sit next to me. My reaction was "Of course you may." As our conversation progressed I sensed that there was something not quite right with him. He continually said, "They are after me!" To which I replied "Who?" He just said "Sssh, they may be listening." At this moment we were called to embark at our designated gate, myself feeling relieved to have escaped from my friend.

Having been shown to my window seat and having made myself comfortable, I was amazed to find that my African gentleman was escorted by the airhostess to the seat next to me. As we approached the runway for take-off my friend got up and ran towards the cabin area, calling as he went "I want to get off!" He was escorted back to his seat by our nice airhostess who reassured him "There is nothing to worry about sir." With his seat belt now fixed, we had lift-off!

Only twenty minutes into the flight he pressed the button for the stewardess. On her arrival he said to her that I was going to kill him. She then asked me if I knew this gentleman. I informed her that my first encounter with him was in the departure lounge. She then turned to him and said "What makes you think that he is going to kill you?" His reply was "He's got a gun." She explained to him that no one could get on board with such a weapon. All seemed to be well for about an hour, when he summoned her again. Accompanied this time by one of the flight officers, he informed them that this time I had a knife! I imagined that the whole plane was looking at me!

After some discussion the officer said to him "He hasn't any weapons. Would you like to sit elsewhere?" His reply was "Yes." He was removed to a seat next to a lady this time, who had been giving me funny looks since our take-off. She started up a conversation with him and all seemed to be well, when he pressed the button again repeating the same comments he had made to the hostess while he was seated next to me, culminating with "She's got a knife too!" On our landing at Doha, the African gentleman was escorted off the plane by two police officers. I learnt later that he certainly had psychiatric problems and was returning home!

CHAPTER 10
"In the Desert"

Being met by Tom at the airport, I was driven back to "Camp Doha." No problems had arisen during my absence and Tom said that he was delighted I was back but there was one small matter he wanted to discuss with me over drinks that evening. It turned out that one of the United Kingdom staff had applied for a position as curator of Bahrain Zoo, subject to his degree being forwarded, which was non-existent. Tom had discovered this in my absence after having taken this man at his word. He was a good storyteller! Following a discussion with this fellow, I convinced him that it was in everyone's best interests that he declined the offer. This he did without any further comment, though not before being severely reprimanded by David Jones, Director of Zoos.

During my discussions with Tom about this keeper, I also brought up the subject of an animal hospital attendant who I noticed had restricted use of his hands, a problem he had had from birth. Tom left the matter with me to find out if anything could be done to help. Having made an appointment to see a specialist at the main hospital in Doha, I accompanied this young man to the consultation. The doctor explained to me that it would require a straightforward operation, costing approximately £1,000. Without hesitation we decided that we would like to have this done. The young man was concerned that he did not have access to this amount of money. However, I told him that this would be my problem. Arriving back at the zoo I spoke to Tom again and suggested that we all had a "whip round" for this operation. The response from the Zoological Society of London staff was amazing and the delighted patient achieved full use of his hands.

In the holding area of the animal hospital, where our young friend worked, there was a Bengal tiger that had apparently been subjected to barbaric dentistry as a young animal. This had developed into a major mouth disorder. After I had discussed the problem with Mike Kock and Tom Begg, enquiries were to be made at the Orthodontic Department of Doha Hospital.

We were given the name of an English dentist who would visit the zoo and examine the sedated tiger. Having completed a full examination of the animal's mouth, he informed us that it was full of infection because the canines had probably been cut off with a hacksaw. This was a fate suffered by young tigers that were kept as family pets, along with having their claws removed. As these large cats grew older they became far too boisterous, such that the owners wanted to donate them to the zoo.

A date was fixed for our large carnivore friend to be taken to Doha Hospital dental unit. The animal was again sedated and laid in the back of the Range Rover, accompanied by myself, the veterinary officer and keeper, with more drugs at the ready in case the feline woke up! Whilst waiting at a set of traffic lights, a vehicle pulled up behind, full of Qataris waving and pulling faces at us. We soon wiped the grin from their faces by dropping the tailgate of the Range Rover. Completely amazed by our occupant, they soon disappeared in the opposite direction.

Arriving at the hospital, we were met by attendants with a large canvas stretcher. This 500 lbs. tiger was manhandled onto the stretcher and taken to the dental unit, where it seemed as though half of the hospital staff had gathered! The animal was checked over again by the vet and then placed in the reclining chair. The dentist's work took four hours, to the amusement of everyone there. On occasions we did wonder if our friend was coming round, but due to the skill of Mike Kock, the animal remained sedated throughout. The operation proved to be a success, with the badly infected teeth being either removed or filled.

One day I received a message from Tom that the vet and I were required to move some cheetahs which were housed in the Emir's palace grounds as part of his private collection. A date was arranged and we set off with equipment which included dog poles and immobilising drugs. After about one and a half-hours drive, we arrived at the entrance to the palace and were confronted by armed soldiers, but after normal security checks we were eventually allowed into the grounds. I was damned if I could see any cheetahs. However, on quizzing the animal attendant he immediately pointed to a pair of pumas, who were not even young animals, but fully grown and not of the best disposition. It was pointed out to him that it would be in no-one's best interest to tackle these animals with a dog-pole. He obviously had no idea of the capabilities of these cats, particularly in a small area. So we suggested alternative methods of moving them - either by being crated or darted. The latter was not acceptable to the powers-that-be at the palace. Therefore only by crate could they be trapped and transported to their new enclosure.

Another similar but less hazardous errand that required our assistance was to catch some Rhesus monkeys in the grounds of a local Sheikh's palace. On this occasion I was accompanied by Frank Wheeler, our small mammals authority from London Zoo, who was mustard at his job! However, despite our best efforts, some of these agile monkeys remained up on the rooftops!

At the palace we were also told that they would like to donate a tank of scorpions to the zoo - but the tank was to remain and only the occupants were to go! Consequently, I quickly delegated this task to my man Frank, who smiled and said "No problem!" Using forceps and what looked like large pickled-onion jars he soon accomplished the task.

Frank was to prove invaluable over the next year with his knowledge and identification of small mammals and reptiles. He was also to spend much of his spare time in the desert looking for the elusive sand-cat, accompanied by a young American lady he had befriended who worked as a bone artist in Doha Hospital. It was part of my job to know at all times what my staff were up to! I often pulled Frank's leg about what he actually did with his spare time in the desert. His reply was to put his index finger to his nose. However, one day a British frigate arrived in port and we were asked to arrange a barbecue in the desert. This went down so well that we were to be invited aboard the ship for lunchtime drinks sometime the following week. One evening whilst driving back from shopping, Frank brought up the subject of our forthcoming lunchtime invitation. I told him that I had not yet made my mind up as to who would be going. His reply was "Well, I am going of course!" "What makes you think that" I replied "when you keep me in the dark about your goings-on in the desert with Betty?" Frank said, "That's outrageous." My reply was "Own up, as it would be a shame if you had to be on duty in the zoo that morning!" The following week five of us, including Frank, went on board the frigate to the petty officer's mess, where we seemed to consume half the ocean! Incidentally, it was interesting to read in the visitors' book that somebody had signed in as "Sheikh rattle and roll", and another of course as "Sheikh my willy."

I was soon to receive a fax informing me of the departure date of a

The giraffes having been released from their crates on arrival at Doha Zoo. (TB)

Giraffe trapped in the moat at Doha Zoo - clearly the author was not keen to get wet too! (TB)

shipment of giraffes from Kenya. A senior Zoological Society of London member of staff, with vast experience of hoof-stock and giraffes in particular, was on his way from London to Kenya, where he would help load up the giraffes which had been kept in a holding area. He would then travel on with the load to Mombassa and finally by ship to Doha, a journey that would take approximately two weeks. In preparation for the arrival of the giraffes, a dividing eight foot bar, the length of the paddock, had to be installed to prevent damage to the trees by the animals, but positioned high enough for their stable-mates the zebras to pass underneath. One of my other concerns was the fact that the giraffes could fall into the six-foot deep moat because it had an unprotected edge into six foot of water but the experts informed me that this would not be a problem. The giraffes arrived on time and were successfully unloaded but remained in their crates for 48 hours, enabling them to get used to their surroundings. Within an hour of their release into the paddock I received a message that a large bull had fallen into the moat. No sooner had we rescued the bull than a cow followed suit, so I decided, before an injury or mortality happened, to arrange for boulders to be placed all around the edge of the moat.

In the next month as things settled down more, we were able to have some time off to explore the environs of Qatar. One such area that repaid investigation was the mango swamp, particularly for our ornithologists, with such species as birds of prey and bee-eaters in evidence. Another worthwhile visit was to Shahaniya, a government breeding area for Arabian oryx, the rare and almost pure white variety. These beautiful animals stand approximately four feet high at the shoulders and weigh in the region of 450 lbs. Living in large herds, these keen-sighted antelope subsist almost entirely on seasonal grasses, leaves and roots of stunted shrubs. They seldom drink and obtain most of their water from the roots and tubers, which they dig up with their hooves.

Another animal that we saw in abundance on our trips was the Arabian camel, often to be seen in the desert in small groups and apparently unattended. These camels were often used for racing, not far from the zoo, displaying the advantages of their longer legs and a lighter body compared to the Bactrian camel. By the way, Arabian and Bactrian camels are capable of inter-breeding, the best combination being a Bactrian male and an Arabian female. The offspring are said to be heavier and more vigorous.

Arabian Oryx at Shahaniya. (TB)

These pleasurable trips were soon to come to an abrupt end as preparations were under way for the opening of the zoo by the Emir at the beginning of April. In the forthcoming weeks I had to maintain our high standards of animal husbandry. The keepers were also to be issued with a new uniform and I had managed to convince the Municipality to introduce a rota, as up to the present time everyone had been working continuously, with little time off.

The keen ornithologists amongst the keepers became involved with the Natural History side of the Doha Museum, having already identified 150 species of birds, moths, reptiles and mammals, thereby supplementing the knowledge of the local workers.

Some of the keepers also participated in the local Doha amateur dramatic society, helping in many ways, from acting to working behind the scenes. The productions drew a cross section of nationalities in the audience. Additional professional productions were put on by well known celebrities such as Jasper Carrot and Chas & Dave, who drew large audiences. Needless to say the tickets were quite expensive!

Tenders had now gone out for the new giraffe house and it was not long before these had been whittled down to three. Eventually a decision was made to accept the middle-priced one. This was to be built under the supervision of J.S. Bonnington, the zoo architects and a St Albans based firm, who had worked for some considerable time in the Middle East.

I spent a lot of time watching the construction of the giraffe house, which seemed to grow quickly! One morning, whilst discussing the drainage system with the architect, I suggested that we continued our conversation over a cup of coffee in the keepers' quarters. Mike Kock joined us but during our discussions we were interrupted by one of the Indian keepers, who informed us that there were men with rifles in the paddocks. Hastily, Mike Kock and I went to investigate. As we approached the lion house we were confronted by two armed soldiers, who blocked our path. Before we could speak, their rifles were raised and we were told to go away. From some distance we could see more armed men, surrounding one man in particular. We found out later that it was the Emir, who had turned up unannounced. His departure was as fast as his arrival!

His next visit was a more formal event - to unveil the plaque commemorating the opening of Doha Zoo. There was a high security presence around the zoo with many officials from this Arab State in

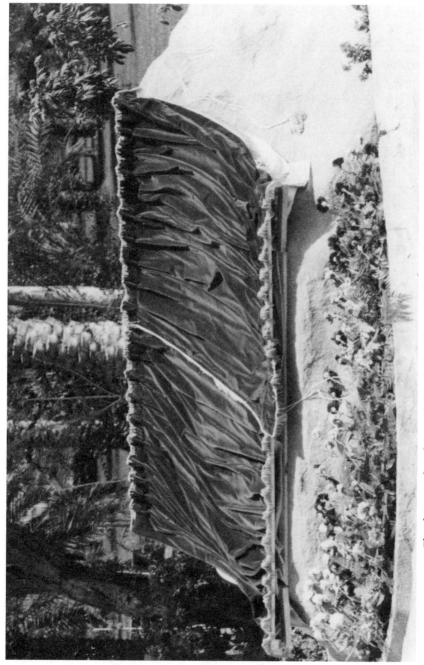

The plaque ready to be unveiled by the Emir to mark the opening of the Zoo gardens. (TB)

111

attendance. The day went faultlessly from beginning to end and, after the departure of the Emir, plans were in place for a non-alcoholic party, which included all Doha Zoo staff. David Jones arrived and presented certificates to the outstanding keepers, who had distinguished themselves in the last 11 months. They were also to receive a book on their particular charges.

My wife Sheila was also able to visit us for a week, spending some of her time meeting and talking with staff in Doha that she knew and, in some cases, had worked with in the Children's Zoo in London. We managed to fit in a trip to Umsaid, which was a town on the coast 25 miles away across the desert, with large sand dunes, frequented by young Arabs in four-wheel drive vehicles and motorbikes. It was not unusual for them to overturn these vehicles on the dunes. On one occasion, whilst bird watching along the seashore, I noticed a Range Rover up to its axles in wet sand with its occupants trying to dig it out! After only about 20 minutes they gave up and left on foot! Consequently it filled up with water as the tide approached. It was still a blot on the landscape when I left Qatar, now minus a few headlights and other valuable accessories.

Tom informed me that before my departure there would be a new intake of Zoological Society of London staff for the following year but that he would stay on for a further year. David Jones also requested that I should stay for another 12 months, but I declined this offer as it had been a hard, albeit fulfilling year and I felt that I needed a break. However, this was a decision I was soon to regret.

My good friend Dr Nabil, to whom I had become very close over the past 10 months, invited me to spend my last evening with him. This started with a feast in his house, an especially prepared Egyptian dinner with, amongst other delights, goats yoghurt made for me by his wife who was in the kitchen the whole evening, before appearing with some cans of seven-up! Having consumed fish, meat, bread and trifle we left to return to the zoo - unable to do our belts up! I thought I was going to bed, but Nabil had other ideas. He wanted me to stay up all night reminiscing over our time together. So we sat by the elephant compound, talking until sunrise.

Noon soon came around, after I had spent all morning shaking hands and saying good-bye to colleagues who had become good friends. Nabil and my outstanding boss Tom drove me to the airport. Having acquired a visa, I was able to have a short stay in Cairo. The flight was uneventful, but

A sphinx at Gaza. (TB)

making my way through customs I was stopped by two gentlemen in plain clothes, who identified themselves as Police officers and subjected me to a close examination. Finally continuing my way through customs and out of the airport, I hailed a taxi.

Back at my hotel I made the acquaintance of an American, with whom I spent a most enjoyable afternoon and evening, returning to Cairo the following morning in time for my flight home. However, at the check-in my two plain clothed friends met me again, this time asking me to accompany them to their office. I was introduced to a Senior Police Officer who asked me to be seated. My continuous interjections that my plane was about to leave were dismissed with a wave of his hand. His line of questioning commenced, "What is your purpose of visit to Cairo?" Answer "Visitor." "Why did you not sleep in your hotel last night?" Answer "Went to Alexandria with an American I met in the Hotel." "What military installations did you visit?" - Pause. "What films did you take?" - Pause. "What did you do with the films after you had taken them?" Answer "I have no films." "Does your American friend have the films?" Answer "He's not my friend." "Do you normally go off with someone you don't know?" Answer "Only if it's a bird!" A smile crept across his face. Whilst this questioning was going on, some kind gentleman was disembowelling my luggage!

My continuous pleas that my plane was about to take off were dismissed with the words "Plane will leave when I say so." Then he said, "Let's be sensible. I am going to give you a sheet of paper and a pen so you may make a full statement regarding your activities in Egypt. Before I leave, tell me about your military service?" My first reaction was "Oh shit!" Thinking that it would inadvisable to mention the Territorials, I said, "I wasn't even a cub!" He said, "What's a cub?" I said "A small bear!" I don't think he was amused and he left the room, with matey still rummaging through my luggage. My statement read as follows: - "I smuggled in six crates of Johnnie Walker whisky which I sold in the market in Cairo!" On his return he read my brief statement; laughing aloud he screwed it up into a little ball and threw it in the waste bin. I then said "What about my plane?" His answer was "Do you like Turkish coffee?" I said "Only if it's made properly." He smiled and said "Of course."

He instructed the luggage vandal, who by now had dissected all my belongings and splayed them over the entire office floor, to get two coffees.

Meanwhile he offered me a cigarette, which tasted terrible, but I continued to puff on it until my friend arrived with our refreshments. Having consumed the coffee I was taken downstairs with some of my socks hanging outside my bag, where they had been hurriedly repacked. They had finally decided I was no threat to their National Security and therefore I could leave. My plane, which was now overdue for take-off, was waiting on the runway. Two armed men took me in a jeep to the awaiting aircraft. As we approached, I could see the passengers looking out of the windows. They must have thought that I was an undesirable and that I was being deported. Having reached the top of the stairs, I turned and saluted the escort! As I walked down the aisle of the plane I could feel people looking at me, or was it just my imagination?

CHAPTER 11
"Return to a Green and Pleasant Land"

Arriving at 9 Chequers Cottages, it was relaxing to sit down with a cup of coffee and reminisce over the 13 months of an amazing, unforgettable experience. Late afternoon, I walked to Whipsnade Common to meet Martin from his school coach. He was delighted to see me and greeted me with "What presents have you for me?" I told him to wait until we arrived home. Rachel came in later from work in Dunstable with a similar greeting. Neither of them looked as though they had suffered from my absence.

By 18.00 hrs, I could not resist the temptation any longer to go to see my elephants at the zoo. Sheila remarked "Can't you wait until tomorrow?" Walking out of the house I called "I won't be long." As I approached the zoo gates I could see Kumara standing on the edge of the moat. Walking past her I said, "How are you, you old bag?" Instantly recognising my voice, she roared and trumpeted, which alerted Katie who came flat out across the paddock. I continued walking, with members of the public looking at me, to the elephant house mess room. Climbing over the small gate I was greeted by Carla who said, "We knew it had to be you, judging from the reactions and commotion of Kumara and Katie!" We entered the compound together, to an unbelievable greeting from the two animals. They were urinating and tossing dung in the air in excitement. This continued for some time before they quietened down.

Colin now joined us, my second in charge, who had been acting Head Keeper the last 13 months. Colin and Carla informed me that Jumbo's attitude had deteriorated towards the staff. He had become very aggressive, a problem I had foreseen and discussed with David Jones some years earlier. We did not have the proper facilities to contain a bull elephant. Although Jumbo was only a forest bull he had done considerable damage to the main barrier. Without a bull yard or a crush to contain him, his life at Whipsnade was limited.

Kumara in playful mood on my return to Whipsnade. (Fr)

A celebration drink with Carla and Colin on my return. (KC)

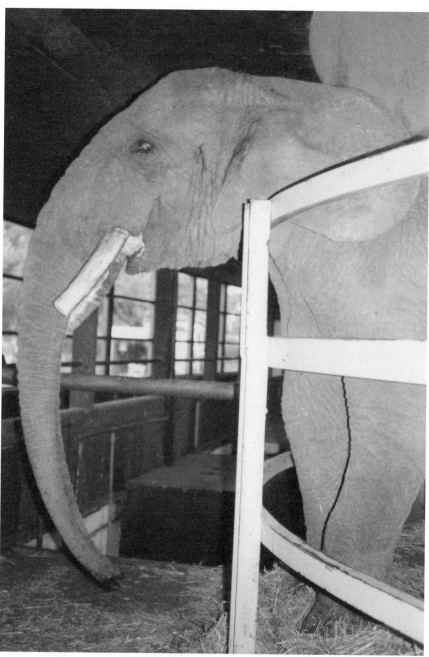

Jumbo in an aggressive mood shown by the wickedness in his eyes. (JF)

Soon afterwards it was decided by Victor Manton, the curator, to make enquiries about relocation for Jumbo. Meanwhile he asked if I would try putting Jumbo in with the two cows. I had great reservations about this introduction, as years earlier Kumara had shown her dislike for the bull. On one particular occasion Kumara had flattened Jumbo in the compound, in her attempt to protect me when he advanced on me aggressively. It was at this time that I felt Jumbo should be separated from Kumara for his own well being. So the bull had been separated now for some time.

However, I treated the request as an order and felt bound to try to reunite the three. I discussed this with Colin and Carla who had similar doubts, but we agreed to have a go when an appropriate time presented itself.

We picked a weekday when public attendance was poor and the elephants were in a quiet mood. Some extra hay was put in the compound and the inter-communicating gate was opened. Jumbo ambled through and we fastened the gate behind him. First of all he walked past Kumara, as if ignoring her, then towards Katie, whose ears immediately came out. She began urinating and looking agitated. She turned towards the bull, who tusked her in her side. Then everything appeared quiet. Turning towards Kumara he adopted the same behaviour. Unlike Katie, Kumara retaliated with her head. Jumbo's legs buckled, but at this point he did not go down. Regaining his balance he bolted towards the gate through which he had come earlier, with Kumara in hot pursuit! Arriving at the gate, through which he could not pass, he just stood urinating and bellowing in fright. Kumara by this time was within striking distance and with one enormous blow to Jumbo's hind quarters, poleaxed him. Without a further thought, I jumped through the barrier positioning myself between them, with Carla shouting "Get out, get out, they'll kill you!" I could feel Jumbo's trembling body behind me and the magnificent Kumara in front of me. I commanded her to back off, and her first reaction was to stand her ground. I repeated the command and this time she backed off and walked away, returning to her bale of hay. Jumbo was then released, back out into the compound and to safety! An exercise not to be repeated! It was not until I returned to the mess room that I began to shake, realising the full enormity of what I had just encountered. This left me with the true sense of respect that this animal obviously had for me.

The 9¹/₂ foot tall Asian elephant, Kumara, trying to take charge of the cleaning up! (E&P)

It was not long after this incident, that one day I found Kumara laying down on her side at the top of the paddock. Having failed to get her onto her feet, I was assisted by a former head keeper of the elephants who was now duty overseer. He said that we must get her into her stable, before the public started to arrive. We achieved nothing at this point. After his departure I decided on different tactics. I called Katie who was apprehensive about leaving Kumara, and she eventually came down for some food. Making a fuss of Katie immediately aroused Kumara's attention. She got up on her feet and slowly walked down the paddock towards us. Kumara was then led into her stable, by which time the vet had arrived.

The normal symptoms for a stomach disorder are loss of appetite, restlessness, alternately lying down and rising up, moving from side to side, opening and closing the mouth frequently, crossing the legs and often striking its side and stomach with its tail or trunk. Overall the animal shows much distress - Kumara had all these signs. The vet who thought that she probably had a form of gastro-enteritis prescribed a course of treatment. The first stage was a large dose of antibiotics given twice daily by injection. After three or four days Kumara grew restless and reluctant to stand for this treatment and as it was dangerous for anyone but myself to administer it, the vet and I decided that the medicine would be given orally. This also proved most difficult, as the elephant would detect which cabbage, banana or orange had the tablets and would stamp on it! This was proving a waste of antibiotics, so I boiled rice and made it into a ball with the tablets inside. By tickling her tongue, I could push the rice ball down her throat, so making sure she took all the pills.

I stayed for two or three nights with her to make sure she kept on her feet, as with some large animals they tend to give up when they have gone down in the stable. Also if they lay down for too long on one side, fluid can build up in the lung, causing more complications! Towards the end of the week Kumara appeared to be on the mend. So I decided to let her lie down for a while. It was during this time that I sat down on the straw next to her with my head resting on her leg. When I awoke it was daylight and Kumara's trunk was in my face as she stood over me. She had obviously manoeuvred me out of the way so that she could rock herself into a position from which to get up. It was an amazing feat, as the stable was only 18 x 18 feet, for such a large animal to achieve without disturbing me and possibly in the dark too!

As time went on the bond between us grew stronger and it was now obvious that I was the one who had total control of her. She still responded well to Colin and Carla, but if any problems arose regarding Kumara, I had to deal with them. On a day to day basis there would often be conflict between her and junior members of staff. Therefore it was important that Colin, Carla or myself always accompanied these staff members.

It was now November 1984 and Carla was asked if she would like to go on a keeper's course, which would mean that one day each week she would have to be released from her work to go to London Zoo for the next two years. She was required to complete a lot of studying, including a project and also practical work, which was assessed by myself. For the project Carla had to design a medium-size cathouse, showing all the workings of the building, an access yard for services, and an outside enclosure. As time went by, it became apparent that she would excel in all areas of her work as a keeper, and she distinguished herself, along with Ken Crouch, another of my keepers on the course. Ken actually came out top overall. However, his fame was to be short-lived.

Having been left on duty in the chimpanzee house, whilst I was at lunch, Ken had just two jobs to carry out in my absence. He had to make up the evening meal for nine chimps and wash out one front den. Having shut the chimps into the race giving them access into the outside enclosure, he should have double-checked that all nine animals were accounted for, before opening the inside den. He said that he had done this, but on my return from lunch I was to learn from my superiors that we had had a chimp running loose in the grounds, though it had now been re-captured by Ken himself. A report had to be submitted to the curator on this incident, after having talked through with Ken as to how the chimp had escaped. He was adamant that the animal had not run past him, but that it must have squeezed through a four-inch gap in the top of the cage. I verified with a zoo owner, a chimp expert in the West Midlands, that this could in fact happen, and my curator accepted this, although we both had our ideas on what we thought had actually happened! It was not long after this that Ken resigned from the zoo and went on to pastures new. I believe he now sells sun beds and repairs flat roofs - some contrast from working with pachyderms!

In 1985 I was pleased to be asked by The Zoological Society of London

A Whipsnade born chimp being hand reared by author and staff. (CT)

Mother with baby chimp. (LZ)

125

to look into the housing and safety aspect of a five-year-old African elephant which was being kept in a barn in the Kent countryside. This request came from Kent County Council, because they had been asked to grant a wild animal licence under the new licensing act to the owner of this animal. They were dissatisfied with a previous report. Apparently the veterinary officer admitted that his knowledge of elephants was limited.

One fresh spring morning, a few days after receiving the request, I headed off into the Kent countryside with my wife Sheila. On arrival at the Council Offices, I discussed the matter with a Council official over a cup of coffee. He drove us out to the farm. We entered a dilapidated barn and were met by the animal's owner, a large man who initially appeared unwelcoming towards us. The first problem that attracted my attention was a freestanding calor gas stove, with a naked flame within six feet of the elephant and its straw bedding. As anyone knows who handles elephants, they love to throw hay over their heads onto their backs, so providing the ideal conditions to start a fire. The structure of the barn itself, comprising old timbers with four inch gaps between, hanging down from the roof, with some of the side timbers coming away, provided draughts for the animal which could also fan any flames into engulfing the barn in minutes. The owner made the comment that the stove was only alight when he was on the premises - but that meant long periods when the elephant would be without heating. The animal was also standing in its urine due to the fact that the drain was completely blocked, which according to the owner had only just happened.

The elephant, a five year old African, was draped in a tarpaulin and stood quite motionless, obviously stressed. I asked for the tarpaulin to be removed, which was done reluctantly and it was apparent to me that the animal was several hundred pounds underweight. Its tail was also completely bandaged and on examination, having removed the bandages, I concluded that there were signs of frostbite. This he denied, claiming that it was an old injury which was present when he bought the elephant. On examination of the animal's diet, which consisted of wastage from the market, it proved totally inadequate for a young growing animal that had probably had a poor start to life anyway and possibly had left its mother before being fully weaned. I also learned that local residents had complained about the elephant being bathed in the village pond. This may have been amusing to the children but not to the Council who considered it a health hazard. I returned to the Council offices, where we took lunch and discussed my findings of the morning. I later understood the application for the wild animal licence had been rejected.

Returning to work the following day, I learned that Meterdali the African elephant that had been on loan to Edinburgh Zoo, was to return to Whipsnade within two weeks. She would be accompanied by Karen, who had been her keeper for the last few years, and transported by a lorry owned by Chipperfield's, who had vast experience in the movement of large animals around the world. The two weeks passed quickly and, with the stable prepared, we awaited arrival. Having released the unlocking bolts of the lorry, one could immediately see the animal through the bars. She appeared slightly nervy, understandably, and agitated in her new surroundings. As soon as she had been released from her leg chains, with the barred door removed and the ramp dropped into position, she was reluctant to walk forwards and down the ramp. With patience and food she was eventually coaxed down the slope into the small compound where she immediately walked over to the dividing barrier to greet Katie, our resident African elephant whom she had not seen for 12 years. Much trumpeting was to take place, with urinating and flapping of ears in excitement. Within an hour one could not imagine that they had ever been parted! Her temperament towards the keepers was excellent, which is always a great advantage when dealing with a large elephant. She settled in easily over the next few months and was re-introduced permanently to Katie without any problems.

Meterdali, however, had a broken tusk which had been a problem for many years and was causing her a great deal of pain. She was examined by Richard Kock, the Society's veterinary surgeon based at Whipsnade. He decided that the tusk would have to be removed as it was probably infected. After some time he made contact with a dentist in North London who had experience in this field. To conduct such an operation we would have to remove the fibre roof of the stable. This would entail hiring a large crane on the morning of the operation; a crane would also be needed to manoeuvre the elephant into position. Large canvas slings would have to be placed around the girth after the animal had been slightly sedated. It would then be lowered onto a straw bed. This was the plan.

This procedure took place a few weeks later. Arriving at work at six a.m. to prepare for the elephant's operation, I ensured all other elephants

Meterdali arrives at Whipsnade none the worse for the journey down from Edinburgh Zoo. (CT)

Old friends re-united - Katie and Meterdali. (CT)

were removed to the outside compound with the exception of our patient, who immediately knew something was up, as did her companions. The team involved in the operation were going to arrive at around nine a.m. The crane had arrived at eight a.m. but would not be operational until the elephant had been slightly sedated. The vet arrived accompanied by myself, and he then administered an injection that would mildly sedate the elephant. Within forty minutes I felt the elephant was quiet enough for the works department to remove the roof. The animal was then hoisted a few feet off the ground and positioned for the operation. Richard Kock, the vet, monitored the breathing and heart rate and gave the O.K to the dentist and his assistant to start work. The first instrument to come out of the bag was a Black & Decker drill! His intention was to drill as far up the centre of the tusk as possible. The flesh around the tusk had to be cut as they intended to remove it in pieces.

During the operation there was continuous bellowing from the elephants outside and my staff had to keep them occupied with fruit and vegetables. These animals were only showing concern for their own. The operation lasted for over four hours from start to finish. The whole of the tusk was removed and was found to be rotten at the top. It was thought that a fracture had taken place some years earlier and there were signs of an infection which must have been causing the elephant pain. After the operation the animal was given the reversal drug and was soon on its feet, the roof having been put back earlier!

I spent the night observing the animal, which appeared still to be in some pain. So early the next morning the vet administered some painkillers. It took several weeks, but eventually the problem cleared up and Meterdali was re-introduced into the paddock with the other elephants.

Katie and Meterdali back together again. (CT)

CHAPTER 12
"With Regret"

At the early age of 16, the aggressive Jumbo was showing signs of musth, just as I had observed in the more mature bull in Qatar. So I decided to go back to the curator to find out if he had anybody interested in taking on the bull. He informed me that he had been in touch with some zoos in Europe who had forest cow elephants, but nothing had yet materialised. For the next two years his behaviour became worse and, with nowhere for him to go, it was decided by the management, with great reluctance, that Jumbo would have to be destroyed. So early one morning the vet arrived and Jumbo was quietly put down, much to the distress of all the staff.

From this sad situation, however, came a completely different approach. I felt we should have a plan to work the elephants. This could take the form of animals pulling logs, carrying and stacking logs in an area constructed for this purpose. This was agreeable with David Jones and would be a good public relations move, as we often encountered criticism regarding the boredom of the elephants and their stereotyped behaviour. This is only too common in animals in zoos all over the world. We also decided to acquire some young stock - three young Burmese elephants for Whipsnade and one for London Zoo. The downside of this was that Kumara would be put on deposit at Chester Zoo. This was devastating news to me in particular, as we had been together for over twenty years and I was also concerned about the effect this would have on Katie, as they had been together since they were babies.

It was suggested that Kumara would have to depart before the new arrivals. In April 1989, a senior member of the keepers' staff at Chester Zoo arrived at Whipsnade to spend one month getting accustomed to Kumara. This proved not to be an easy task. The keeper from Chester had his own thoughts on handling Kumara. I soon enlightened him that these ideas could be a short cut to disaster, as he would have to woo Kumara and this would take time. Each day for the following month he would spend many

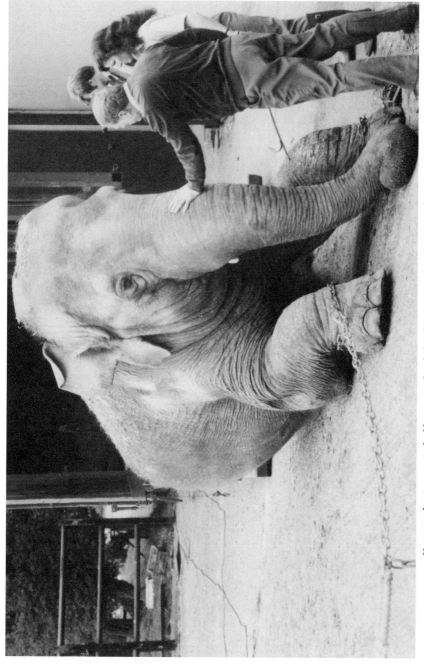

Kumara, having a mind of her own, decided to lie down rather than go off to Chester Zoo. (Fr)

hours with Kumara and myself. Finally May 2nd arrived, the day of Kumara's departure to Chester Zoo. At 08.00 hrs a Chipperfield lorry arrived and with twenty staff on hand from the zoo we set about winching Kumara inch by inch up the ramp and into the lorry. All went well to start with and then half way up the ramp she decided to step off it. This meant that the winch cable had to be slackened off to get Kumara into position again. Having done this, she laid down! With a lot of coaxing and pulling, we managed to get her on her feet again. Unlike the rest of the keeping staff, Colin, Carla and myself were in close contact with three tonne of elephant and not once did she show any aggression towards us. This was incredible considering the stress the animal was under. Gradually Kumara was coaxed into going backwards, up the ramp and into the lorry. Once she was securely fastened in the lorry she was made a fuss of and we were soon on our four-hour journey to Chester Zoo. On arrival the animal was somewhat apprehensive about her new surroundings, but was led out of the lorry by Colin and myself. She soon settled into her new quarters and it was decided that Colin would remain with Kumara for one month. I kept in touch with Colin as to how things were progressing. I was under the impression that progress was slow and that Kumara did not get on with the rest of the elephants there. Colin returned after one month, not totally convinced that all was well.

In late May 1989 I left for Burma with Brian Harman, the Head Keeper of Elephants from London Zoo, and our mission was to select the four young cow elephants. These animals were to be purchased by the Zoological Society of London through a Dutch animal dealer by the name of Frans Van Den Brink whom we were to meet at Bangkok airport before a connecting flight to Burma - to a small airport, outside Rangoon which only received two flights from Bangkok each week. There was a presence of armed police and officials. As the baggage was taken from the small aircraft it soon became apparent that our luggage was not there! After some difficulty with the customs officials, trying to explain the predicament we were in, they eventually telephoned through to KLM in Bangkok. They told us our luggage had probably been left on the previous aircraft and gone to the Philippines! They suggested that on our return to Bangkok we should check the lost property office!

Having now accepted our fate we proceeded through customs, which without Franz would have been extremely difficult due to all the

Kumara arriving at Chester Zoo. (CT)

Kumara with John in stable at Chester Zoo. (CT)

bureaucracy. We were met outside by an official from the Burmese Timber Co-operative who own a large proportion of the timber elephants. We were taken to our hotel which was within 500 yards of Rangoon Zoo. We were made familiar with the hotel regulations and meal times, which had been orchestrated around an imposed curfew. This curfew came into play at seven thirty p.m. until eight thirty a.m., which meant that between these hours nobody could walk the streets, and if anyone did so they stood a good chance of being shot! We settled into our hotel bungalows with a lovely view of the lake with its water lilies, lush vegetation and bird life. On the surface this beautiful place had an air of tranquillity, but appearances were deceptive. For example red rusty water gushed out of the showerhead, followed by much gurgling and clanking of pipes. This indicated that this bungalow had not been used for some time, maybe due to the fact that one could only visit Burma when on a business venture.

The next day we were met by the Senior Veterinary Officer from Rangoon Zoo who proceeded to give us a guided walk around the gardens. Eventually we ended up at the elephant house, where some young cow elephants were tethered to rings in the ground. These animals were for my inspection, each one having its own mahout. We had about six animals from which to choose. I was unimpressed with this particular batch. Some had broken tails, some split toenails and some appeared aggressive. Also I felt that some of these animals were younger than we had been led to believe, with the possibility that they had been taken away far too early from their mothers. This was disputed.

Unimpressed by this motley bunch they had brought to show us, Brian and I said that we would like to view some other specimens. Two days later we were taken to a holding area outside Rangoon. The animals here were a different kettle of fish! So we selected eight elephants to be brought down to the zoo for closer inspection. I think at this point the Burmese officials and Frans, the animal dealer, realised that they were dealing with two men who had years of experience with elephants, maybe not in the wild, but certainly in zoos. We observed and studied this group for about a week before picking out four young cows of approximately five to six years of age. Documents were produced proving their authenticity as captive-bred - a requirement for the Endangered Species Act. Looking back, I realise that we had no real proof of this, as the documentation that we had seen could have fitted any of the cows we had viewed.

View from our accommodation in Burma. (BH)

138

Some elephants for my inspection, being put through their paces by Frans. (BH)

Having chosen four elephants I decided that, when these animals eventually arrived in Holland, it was imperative that I would be able to identify them. I therefore set about measuring their height, girth, trunk, tail and noting any distinguishing features that would make them instantly recognisable to me. I made sketches of ears and skin pigmentation and any unusual markings. We spent the next week seeing the animals being put through their paces, which included their being ridden by the mahouts, lying down on command, lifting a leg up for close foot inspection and raising a trunk for a mouth examination.

The only problem with this was that all these commands were in Burmese, so these had to be learnt during the evenings in curfew time! When we felt reasonably confident we reported to our charges. Needless to say there was little or no response initially, probably due to our cockney accents! During these training sessions Brian was videoing our progress! Having always handled elephants from the ground, it was to prove a new and painful experience riding them! The Burmese, being of slight stature unlike myself, and also very supple, made it look easy. One realises one's limited knowledge when working with such experts in this field.

In our leisure time we spent hours walking around the market in Rangoon purchasing carvings of elephants and we managed to obtain a copy of "Burmese Timber Elephant" by U Toke Gale. The author was a retired Burmese forester with many years' experience and he had written the book from first hand knowledge. In other free time we admired the architecture in Rangoon, which reflects the influence of British, Dutch and of course Japanese, but one felt that one could not observe at great length, due to the presence of the military everywhere. We were also invited to a garden party given by a prominent official. The garden was floodlit, the food was excellent and the icing on the cake was a bottle of Johnnie Walker, placed on our table, obviously with Europeans in mind! We furthermore witnessed a Burmese wedding with all its colour and jollity and we were given a guided tour of The Golden Temple. The hospitality and friendliness of the Burmese is something I will never forget.

Our time here too soon came to an end. The day before we left, Frans dealt with the shipping and all the legalities for the elephants' departure. Departing from Rangoon airport by Bangladeshi Airways was an experience in itself. Just after the announcement for passengers to return to their seats and fasten seatbelts, they did exactly the opposite - grabbing

Crocodile Farm in Bangkok. (BH)

their bags and making their way to the front of the aircraft, causing mayhem. After a while the airhostesses persuaded them to return to their seats. Within one hour we arrived in Bangkok.

I was soon making enquiries about our lost luggage. Eventually we were directed to a lost luggage holding area. After some searching we were successful, though the locks had been forced open and the bags had obviously been searched. It appeared that nothing had actually been taken, though, and we later found that it was standard procedure to check all lost luggage for drugs or any other undesirable substances.

We spent a week in Thailand in a very prestigious hotel. Frans had business to conduct whilst in the country, so we took the opportunity to visit some animals, such as those at the crocodile farm with its 30,000 exhibits ranging in size from a few inches to ten feet. We saw a display with a man wrestling with a crocodile and many other sideshows, including a crocodile skin shoe shop! This place was a haven for animal rights organisations!

An elephant display was impressive. There was lots of noise and gunfire with the elephants engaged in mock battles, with their riders on their backs. We saw riders fall from their charges and the elephants were trained to take fright and run off. This battle lasted about forty minutes and was then followed by a display of capturing wild elephants. Approximately 10 to 15 elephants were released into a large compound. These were to be the wild ones and had been trained to act as such. Three or four elephants with their mahout riders then entered the compound and they had in their hands long poles with nooses on the end. They also had lots of ropes for securing each animal once it had been captured. The idea was to secure the rear leg of an elephant in the noose. Once this had been achieved, another mahout on his mount would assist this rider. They would then secure the "wild" elephant between two trained ones, enabling them to escort it to the stockade, where in reality it would then undergo a programme of training, which varied in length, depending on the age of the individual elephant. In my opinion, this was experiencing elephants being worked to perfection. On speaking to the mahouts afterwards, they informed me that some of the tasks we had observed had taken months to perfect.

The following day we visited the local zoo and were given a conducted tour by the curator, who suggested that we might like to view the Palace Stables, which he said he could arrange, much to our delight. In the afternoon we were taken to the Palace grounds and introduced to the manager. We were shown a variety of elephants, some of which had been man killers in their working life. We also saw some with blue eyes, which neither of us had seen before. The "pièce de resistance" was the King's sacred white elephant, which had been captured many years earlier in the forests of Thailand. We learnt that all white elephants, on discovery, have to be reported to the appropriate authority and the King has to be informed. All the elephants, including the white one, were of unpredictable behaviour. This could have been due to the fact that they were very restricted in their movements, being chained on all four legs. Asked if they had any exercise, the manager was non-committal. So we both drew our own conclusions. Nevertheless this was a unique experience for Brian and myself.

Back at work in England the following day, we had a meeting with David Jones about the elephants we had purchased. We told him that the elephants would be leaving Burma within two weeks on a Burmese ship, accompanied by two mahouts and a vet. The shipment consisted of about 20 elephants, including a mother and baby, bound for Rotterdam. The journey took 31 days and we were informed two days before they docked of their imminent arrival in Rotterdam. This would give Brian and myself time to reach Holland to meet the ship.

Preparations were now under way in the elephant compound at Whipsnade to receive these animals. Tethering rings had to be inserted into the concrete yard under the supervision of Grant Guild, the Works Department foreman, an old friend, who had done lots of work in the elephant house. He often gave me priority over other sections, which left him open to criticism by those who felt he favoured my requests. The fact that his lovely wife adored elephants, and spent a considerable time videoing them, had nothing to do with it!

The time soon came for us to depart for Holland. David suggested that we should take the zoo Volvo and drive to Harwich to catch the ferry to The Hook. This we did, arriving at 06.00 hrs. I then drove us into the middle of Amsterdam, in the rush hour, which was quite nerve wracking, being out of practice driving on the wrong side! Eventually I had to stop and ask directions to the zoo where we had arranged to meet Frans. On arrival there we presented ourselves at the main gate, where we were introduced to the zoo manager. He told us that Frans was going to be an hour late, so we were invited to walk around the zoo gardens.

On arrival, Hans suggested that we should follow him in his car to his farm in Soëst near Amersfoort, which took just over an hour to reach. There we were introduced to his wife Elli and his two daughters, his driver and handyman Mark and last but not least Maria his secretary, who reminded me of an SS interrogator. As one got to know her she was not a bit like that. She told us that we had accommodation in a small, family run hotel just two minutes away in the car. Frans told us he had confirmation that the elephants would be docking in Rotterdam in three days. He showed me the holding area where the 10 animals would be housed and I suggested that he should arrange for 20 tethering rings to be installed immediately, as there were no facilities to contain these animals. He organised for a blacksmith contractor to do the work the next day. When this was successfully completed we were ready to receive our load.

Early the next morning we set off for the docks with two large low loaders, one driven by Mark and the other by Buck, who was a contractor who had done work for Frans in the past. Arriving at the dockyard we were met by Customs Officials and given an escort to the ship. We could see that the walkway was in position and Frans, Brian and myself were beckoned aboard. We were greeted by the Captain and his First Officer, who suggested that we might like some refreshment while the Customs Officials searched the ship for any unwanted goods entering Holland! With everything in order we were given the OK to start unloading. Halfway through this the dockers disappeared, apparently for their tea break! It did not seem to matter that one crate was left suspended in the fresh air! Fifteen minutes later they returned to work. Four hours later the whole shipment was unloaded, with some of the elephants departing for various zoos in Holland.

As promised, the Timber Corporation had sent three mahouts with our shipment, who accompanied us in the lorry. This was a great adventure for them as this was their first time outside Burma. We had two police motorcyclists as outriders, who cleared the traffic ahead all the way back to the farm. A huge crane unloaded the crates. This having been accomplished, the crane was moved away from the area so as not to frighten the elephants. We then set about undoing all the nuts and bolts. As each crate was opened a mahout entered and climbed onto the elephant's neck and rode it out. This was an amazing feat as these animals had been contained with restricted movement for thirty-one days. This was to show yet again the control and experience these mahouts have achieved. Once all the elephants were out of their crates, they were exercised in the small paddock and given water to drink. We then proceeded to check the animals over and identify our charges. There were no visible signs of injury sustained during their long trip and they appeared to be in good order. A fax was sent to London Zoo saying the animals had arrived safely.

Over the next two days, under the supervision of the mahouts, we put the elephants through their paces and familiarised ourselves with the Burmese commands once again. All appeared to be going well until we received a fax from Zoological Society of London stating that they wanted the elephants checked for worms by the Dutch Veterinary Department in Utrecht. This did not go down very well with Frans as he said this was not in the contract. After a couple of days the temperature between my

Elephants being unloaded from the ship in Rotterdam. (FVB)

Mahout riding elephant out of the crate. (FVB)

After 47 days on the water these captive bred Indian elephants finally made it safe and sound to the animal farm in Soëst, Holland. (FVB)

immediate boss and myself had deteriorated somewhat and whilst in conversation on the telephone one evening I was ordered to return to London. My reply was "It's a bad line, I can't hear what you are saying." Whereupon he hung up!

Frans had been listening to the conversation and told me to ignore this instruction as he would speak directly to David Jones. He then went on to say that he would like me to go with Mark and deliver a young bull elephant to a zoo in East Germany the next day. Brian declined to go with us and said he would "hold the fort" until my return. He did wonder what reaction he would get from my boss when he enlightened him on my whereabouts!

The next day Mark and I set off on our long drive to East Germany and East Berlin Zoo, a twenty one-hour drive. Things seemed to be going well as we drove along the autobahn when there was a banging noise coming from the rear of our lorry. Mark pulled off the road into a service station and then set about checking our load. Finding nothing loose on the outside of the vehicle and that all locking bolts seemed to be in place, the crate appeared to be OK. However, on opening the inspection door which is normally used for watering and feeding, I could see one chain on the elephant's hindquarters had come undone. Telling Mark of my findings a grin came over his face and he said "I'm just the driver, you're the elephant expert!" With some apprehension whilst talking to and patting the animal, I climbed inside. I could sense that he was not a happy jumbo and he immediately tried to kick me with his free leg. My initial reaction was "Oh shit!" After some minutes, which seemed like hours, I managed to get the chain around his foot. With the last turn in the U-bolt, I knew I had succeeded. The elephant was still grumbling as I climbed back through the small hole. Mark, who was standing outside, said, "You look as though you could do with a fag!"

We decided this was a good opportunity to water and feed the elephant and ourselves! After we had eaten, we climbed into our sleeping bags in the compartment provided, for two to three hours sleep. After about an hour I woke to find my feet wet. Putting my hand down inside the sleeping bag I discovered it was not only my feet that were wet but most of my body. Calling to Mark, who was on the lower bunk, I asked if he was soaked. He said that he was fine, but commented that the roof above me had some missing rivets and that water could come in! It was at this point that I decided to give up trying to sleep. I put the light on and got dressed and sat in the cab, leaving Mark still asleep. Just before dawn he emerged and we had a brew up. I checked the elephant, gave him water and then we continued on our way, driving across Germany and experiencing some beautiful scenery. Stopping at the East German border we decided to have a nice "steak and veg" which was advertised on a board. Having consumed the steak, I was to discover later that it was horsemeat! Nevertheless it went down very well.

Returning to the truck we drove to the barrier. After some documentation, we were directed to a searching area where guards and dogs checked the vehicle. The dogs were somewhat apprehensive and pulled in the opposite direction to that in which the handler wanted them to go, completely refusing to obey any commands, which did not amuse the guards! Being on my own with the guards whilst Mark was seeing to the paper work, there was no communication possible. So, I just opened the back of the lorry so they could see the contents! A smile appeared across the faces of the guards and the dogs were put back in their boxes and the weapons were leaned against the wall. They then requested to feed the elephant. So having been supplied with fruit and vegetables, they proceeded to throw them through the bars. Due to their enthusiasm it was some time before we were once again on our way, encountering some of the worst roads I have ever driven on.

Arriving at the zoo in the middle of the afternoon, I reported our presence to the main office. A charming man who was the Director of the zoo soon greeted me. Before any unloading we were invited to have gateaux and coffee in the zoo restaurant. After this we decided the best way to unload was to reverse the lorry through a very narrow gap, expertly achieved by Mark, still leaving us 200 yards from the elephant house. Once again, a smile appeared on Mark's face as he reminded me that he was the driver and, as the elephant man, the rest was up to me. I asked the Director if it would be possible to clear some of the general public away from the immediate area - which he directed somebody to do. Gingerly, I opened the crate, releasing the chains one by one, and took hold of the elephant's ear in one hand and a hook in the other. The animal seemed quiet and unperturbed by its new surroundings and giving him Burmese commands to walk on, he did so out of the crate. We covered the 200 yards quite quickly and we were soon into a confined area, much to my relief. I escorted the elephant into the stable and chained him up, much to the astonishment of the Director and keepers. I was asked if he would lie down on command, which he did without hesitation. Overall they were most impressed and delighted with their new charge.

During the meal in the evening, with the zoo officials, I jokingly said to the Director "any chance of Diplomatic immunity?" Laughingly he asked "Why?" I said "I might be in the dog house!" He replied "Most people are happy to leave East Germany. I have never been asked by an Englishman if he could stay!"

After a very interesting evening, Mark suggested that we should start our long drive back to Holland. It did not take me long to drop off to sleep, only to be awakened by the driver shaking my arm, saying "We have been pulled over by the Polizei." I soon realised that it was getting light, so I had actually been asleep for some hours. My first thought was that it must be breakfast time! Then the word "Polizei" came back to me. There, as large as life, standing next to his motor cycle was the officer. He was soon into deep conversation with Mark, whose German was excellent. He examined the tachometer and decided the distance we had travelled was in excess of that allowed by the existing legislation. Therefore Mark was fined on the spot. As we drove away, Mark commented that this was quite normal, but admitted that he had put his foot down!

Arriving back in Soëst we briefed Frans on the trip, over a large Johnnie Walker, and then he dropped the bomb that my boss was due the following day. On returning to my hotel room I found Brian lying on the bed reading a book. He looked up and said, "You're in trouble. I tried to cover for you, but in the end I had to tell him where you had gone. Needless to say your boss was not amused. He is coming out tomorrow!" I told Brian that Frans had already imparted that information to me. The following lunchtime my superior arrived, apparently in a good mood! But I knew it was only the smile on the face of a tiger! Being a veterinarian, he said that he would take the blood samples himself and would take them to Utrecht to the veterinary department. This he did. The results came back within three to four days and proved to be clear. He made no comment on my absence from Holland and we made arrangements for the four elephants to go by lorries, on the ferry to Dover. A senior mahout and a vet accompanied the animals to the United Kingdom. As part of the contract they would remain in England for two weeks. Arriving in Dover by mid-day, the customs officers directed the lorries to a particular area where they could look inside and where we could also give the elephants a drink. There appeared to be more paperwork in England about the mahout and the vet, than the elephants! After the officers were satisfied, we were on our way and arrived in Whipsnade in the late afternoon.

It was a lovely sunny day and as we came in through the main gate there were lots of zoo staff present around the elephant house, including my wife Sheila, daughter Rachel and the Director, David Jones. Once the lorries were in position we started to unload the four young elephants, much to the delight of my staff, particularly Carla and Colin. As the elephants were led out, they were chained in the yard to be inspected by David Jones and other officials. They seemed happy with our purchases and the press were there taking pictures and wanting information regarding the authenticity of these animals. They wanted information as to where they had come from, whether or not they were captive-bred and what was the justification in bringing them to England in the first place. It was at this point that David Jones took over the conversation, explaining that this marked the beginning of a new breeding programme, where bulls would be used from other zoos in the country.

All went well for the next couple of months, having been told that I had 12 months to finish training the elephants. We had arrived at the stage where the elephants could come out of the elephant house into the main part of the park and be ridden by all my staff, due to the expertise of my Burmese colleagues. In addition we had used a local man in the village, a harness maker, to come up with some ideas for a harness that would be suitable for the elephants so as to pull logs which had ring attachments for chains to be fitted. After measuring all the elephants individually, he said that he was confident that he could make the harnesses. Having agreed a price with the zoo, he set about the task. After some weeks he arrived with the harnesses for us to try out and after some minor alterations we were ready for the off! Once the elephants were familiar with their harnesses, we attached some large chains either side. One member of staff walked by the side of the animal while the other member of staff followed up behind with the chains, gently tapping the elephant's flanks. This accustomed the animal to the feel of the chains. As far as I was concerned, things were progressing well.

My first indication of any problems was to come in the form of

Refreshing bath by John on arrival at Whipsnade. (CT)

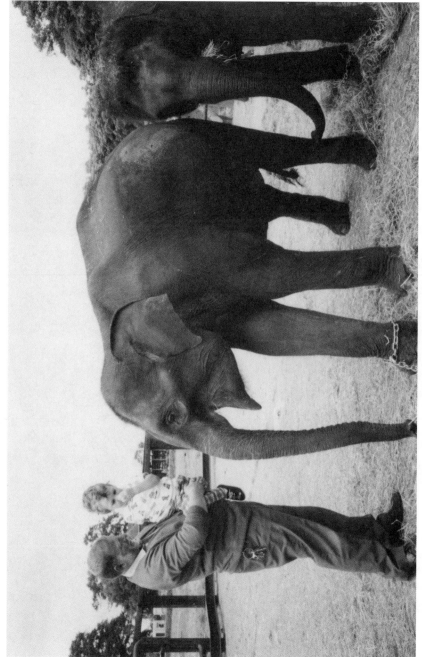

Introducing one baby to another! (CT)

Training starts - Carla and Sally showing great panache. (CM)

A brief rest from training. (CM)

Training session to accustom the elephant to the noise and feel of the chains on the body. (LZ)

Harness being worn by Luca - made by local craftsman, Gwilym Evans. (CT)

It's all too much, boss! (CT)

comments being passed on the names I had chosen for the elephants, namely: - Luca, Kahli and Anna. This was followed by a memo stating that there would be an elephant show for Easter in three months time, which in my opinion was out of the question. After some long discussions with the management, I had to make the hardest decision of my life which would affect my family and my whole way of life. For the past 32 years I had wanted to do nothing else in my life, except to work with animals, and so it was to take 12 months before I finally resigned, with great sadness and regret, from the Zoological Society of London.

Without the support of the Church, our many friends in Whipsnade and surrounding villages, and my family, who all felt upset at the way I was treated, I would have been unable to cope with the stress that I had to endure in the months to come.

The period that followed was extremely difficult and a lot of soul searching ensued. Having always believed that one should have the courage of one's convictions, I had now put this into practice, but with this decision I threw away over 30 years of the work I loved, and subjected myself to much pain, which I still feel to this day.

CHAPTER 13
"A New Start"

My first encounter with work other than with animals, was to be offered a job by the church organist, who was bursar at the local Preparatory School, as Assistant Groundsman. During my time here I learnt new skills, tractor driving, preparation of cricket pitches, rugby fields and the maintenance of the school pool. My other duties included tea-making, keeping the mess room tidy and cleaning the workshop floor.

However, within a few months, I received a phone call from my old friend Frans who enquired whether I would be interested in a job, which entailed a large shipment of elephants from Burma. Initially my answer was "Yes", but I explained that I would have to ask for leave from my new job. I did wonder, going to work the next morning, what the reaction would be to my request, having been there only a short time. The first person I approached was the foreman who said he would speak to the bursar at his normal 09.00 hrs meeting. On his return the foreman informed me that the bursar would see both of us at 11.00 hrs. Nervously, at 11.00 hrs I reported with my boss to the office and immediately was made to feel at ease. Grenville Williams, whom I had known for many years through Whipsnade church, was extremely helpful and understanding and agreed instantly to 15 days unpaid leave to "complete my venture."

Having discussed this with Sheila, we agreed that this would be an opportunity to work once again with pachyderms. Within a week I received my brief from Frans. It read that I would meet his representative in Cairo at six a.m. in the morning, having already picked up two large cases which contained fan heaters from Holland. The idea was then to drive with his agent from Cairo to the Suez Canal where I would meet the ship in the Red Sea and sail with the elephants to the port of Rotterdam.

The morning soon arrived for my departure to Luton airport. The early evening flight had been put on hold due to some technical trouble and we were advised that our flight would be late leaving. Having eventually found somebody that actually knew what was happening, I explained my predicament about having a connecting flight in Holland. She informed me that she would pass on my comments. I was directed, with the other waiting passengers, to the coffee lounge where we were to wait until we were eventually called after 40 minutes to board the aircraft. Arriving at the top of the boarding staircase, I was greeted by a stewardess who asked me if I was the gentleman with the connection in Holland. I replied "Yes." Peering over her shoulder was a man in uniform who introduced himself at the Captain of the flight. He said "Not to worry sir, I'll put it in top gear and have you there in 40 minutes." He was true to his word.

Having landed and retrieved my holdall, I set about looking for Frans. It was not long before I found my large friend, standing with two enormous suitcases on a trolley. He informed me that there was not any time to waste and that we must hasten to the check-in for my flight to Cairo. It was not until I lifted my cases from the trolley that I realised that my 30 years of weight lifting had not been in vain! Frans laughed as he handed me the paperwork and suggested that I should fit the heaters to blow warm air onto the elephants, before we reached the colder waters of the Bay of Biscay.

An uneventful flight to Cairo followed, arriving at six in the morning. As I made my way with my heavy cases towards the customs area I knew what was coming before he said "Could you put the cases onto the table, sir?" With a deep breath and a bit of bully-beef I managed to get both of the cases onto the table, which seemed much higher than a normal table, or maybe it was just early in the morning and I did not feel very strong! Then came the request to open the cases. Looking bewildered and scratching his head, he said there would be £70 import charge. I informed him that the two combined were not worth £70 as they were second hand, so maybe he would like to keep them. He immediately dropped his price to £50 and after some haggling we settled on £20, much to the relief of the other waiting passengers behind me in the queue!

As I made my way to the designated area to meet the agent, there was no one to be seen. So I decided to walk with my heavy load to the refreshment area, where I hoped to find a telephone. Having found a telephone, I tried to phone Frans to tell him that my escort had obviously vanished into thin air! My call was unsuccessful so I telephoned Sheila, getting her out of bed, to get her to telephone Frans. This was to prove ineffective, so I had to use my own initiative to arrive at the Suez Canal. In the meantime I had to pay a visit to the washroom, having left my cases at the top of the stairs, thinking only a weight lifter would steal them. Taking my holdall with me to the washroom I was approached by two undesirable looking fellows who informed me that they wanted some money! A short fracas took place within the loo, and I left, with them sitting on the floor mumbling in Arabic! My number was not up today!

Eventually I found somewhere to sit and have a coffee and gather my thoughts. I was approached by a man in his early 40's who asked me if he might join me at my table. He then asked me if I was English or American. Quite affronted by this I said "English of course, old boy!" He asked me what I was doing in Cairo and if I required a guide. I told him that I would not bother to speak Arabic as his English was so good! I told him about the predicament I was in and that I had to reach the Suez Canal by that evening. He asked me if I had any documentation relating to the Port Authorities at Suez. I handed him the relevant information and he went away and made some telephone calls. Eventually he returned, grinning from ear to ear. He told me that the ship carrying the elephants would be arriving at The Red Sea at about six p.m. that evening and that Van Den Brink's agent had booked me into The Red Sea Hotel at Suez. That in itself was fine but I still had to get there. My companion confided in me that he was once an officer in the Egyptian Army and of course totally trustworthy, and that he and his friend could drive me in his taxi across the desert to my destination. All this for a mere 100 dollars. After some bargaining I got him down to 80 dollars with a drive around Cairo thrown in. He told me that the drive would take over three hours to The Canal. He disappeared for 20 minutes, returning with a friend and a vehicle that looked as though it had had an argument with a JCB! They took my heavy cases from me and I clambered into the back of the car. After a drive of over two hours, taking in the sights of Cairo, my driver stopped to ask a policeman the directions for the Suez Canal. My response to this enquiry was amazement as I thought he knew where we were going. Eventually the policeman set us off on the correct route.

After an hour we were well into the desert and my driver continually suggested that I should close my eyes and go to sleep! This I was not keen to do after my encounter earlier in the day! I could see the warning lights flashing on the dashboard which indicated to me that we were overheating. When I mentioned this, it was dismissed as not a problem. Now, two hours into our journey, there had been no visual indication that we were heading for the Canal. So were their intentions to mug me? Was this the reason they wished me to go to sleep? We were gradually becoming aware of a large military build-up in the desert either side of us. This made me less apprehensive towards my two friends. The military presence was due to the trouble in Kuwait. It was not long after this that I saw my first sign "Suez Canal Ahead", which made me feel much more at ease with my driver and his mate and the fight to keep awake suddenly seemed less important. After a further hour of desert driving we arrived at The Red Sea Hotel to find that a reservation had been made for me in the name of Frans Van Den Brink's agent, with a message saying "Sorry I missed you in Cairo." Delighted with my two companions who had been true to their word, I gave them their 80 dollars and a handsome tip, with which they were delighted.

Having deposited my luggage in my room, I picked up my towel and trunks and set off towards the canal, where I had a refreshing dip. After this I made my way to the Port Authority Offices who informed me that my ship would be docking just outside the canal in the Red Sea at 18.00 hours. I learnt that I would be informed by the Customs Office at my hotel. Having settled this in my mind, I returned to the hotel and a siesta. I was awakened two hours later by a knock on the door by a hotel steward who told me that I was expected in the hotel lounge for a coffee with the agent.

Arriving in the lounge I was met by my elusive guide, who apologised profusely for having missed me in Cairo, but praised my initiative in getting to the Canal. He also told me that Frans had spoken very highly of me and that he was sure the shipment would be in very good hands. After our coffee we proceeded to the restaurant for dinner whereupon I consumed a large T-bone steak with a side salad and alcohol-free wine. During dinner he mentioned that there might be a slight problem with the customs regarding the heaters, but that we would be meeting a Senior Customs Officer in the lounge after our meal. Retiring to the lounge, I was introduced by my agent to the Customs Official, a handsome tall man who explained to me that he was Pharaohic and proud of it! As we talked it soon became apparent to me that some of my money which was for expenses was to end up in his pocket, due to the fact that I did not have an export licence. I told him that I did not have an import licence either and that I had met a gentleman like him before in Cairo who had also required my money! After some haggling we agreed on a price and the "cloak and dagger" trip to the docks was to take place at 22.00 hrs. He told me that I would be met by a black limousine that would take me to the Customs Gate at the docks. As arranged, we set off for the docks, driving straight through the gates to the water's edge, where we climbed aboard the tug which proceeded to the large ship moored a mile offshore.

After a bowl of rice for breakfast, next I went to meet the Burmese vet and the mahouts, who then took me forward to inspect the elephants in the large crates on deck. They all appeared to be in good order considering they had been on board for 16 days. They appeared to have adequate food supplies and had been mucked out twice a day and the vet was satisfied with their condition.

My first night's sleep proved to be very restless. This was because my mattress was alive with man-eating bugs! When I woke up I was covered in dried blood! I decided not to use the bed in future, but to sleep in the armchair. At breakfast I commented on my findings to the first officer who said that it must be due to my lily-white skin!

Each morning thereafter, I inspected the elephants and spent considerable time talking to the mahouts and the vet. On occasions, I found myself mucking out, as the mahouts were often seasick. Sometimes the movement of the ship had an adverse effect on the elephants, proving that they too were seasick.

During dinner one evening I commented on the tenderness of the meat. The Captain remarked that he had heard from the medical officer that maybe my diet was insufficient and that some meat would not go amiss. Smiling he said, "So you enjoyed the monkey?" We picked up some fresh meat when we stopped over in India and also some snake and fresh-water eels. I must say that when one only has rice three times a day, any meat tastes like beef!

It was now nearing the time to liaise with the electrician on the fitting up of the warm air blowers, now that we were approaching the cooler waters of the Gibraltar Straits and the North Atlantic. The positioning of the heaters was not easily accomplished, as they had to be out of reach of the elephants' trunks, and in some crates there was more than one elephant! The crates were extremely large and had been completely lined with plywood to keep the heat in and the bad weather out. If the weather conditions deteriorated severely we also had tarpaulins that would completely cover the containers. After several days of re-positioning the heaters, we found the appropriate place which was beneficial to the elephants and for any maintenance that was required. Now having reached the North Atlantic, the heaters had to be in operation 24 hours a day. I also kept a close watch on the temperature within the containers. I had decided to leave the elephants on deep-litter until we reached Rotterdam, in the hope of generating more heat until we docked in about three days time.

No sooner had we docked than the Customs Officials with their sniffer dogs came on board. They went through the ship with a fine toothcomb looking for any illegal substances. Once they had finished their search they informed us that we could start unloading. After normal unloading delays Frans arrived a little late and told me about the animal rights people who were protesting outside the docks. These people were moved along by the police as we drove out of the docks. We had an uneventful drive to Frans' holding area, in a suburb of Soëst. As we approached the main gates there were more animal rights people protesting with banners. We drove through peacefully and no incidents took place. I could sympathise with their views but these animals were going to Holland irrespective of whether I had been on board or not and therefore I had no feelings of guilt. I had simply made their journey more comfortable. Having unloaded the elephants and completed the administration with the local authority and the Ministry Vet, it was time to retire to the hotel, retrieve my land legs, and have a hot bath, before phoning Sheila to tell her that I had arrived safely in Holland.

Over dinner that evening Frans asked me if I would consider staying for a further four days to take one young elephant to Switzerland, one to Germany and two to Paris zoo. I agreed to the Germany and Paris journeys and said I would find an experienced elephant keeper to do the delivery to Switzerland. The following morning I made a telephone call to Carla who had worked with me at Whipsnade for 10 years and asked her if she would be interested in the job. She immediately agreed and I gave all her details to Maria - Frans' secretary.

After a few days rest on the farm I set off with Mark and one female elephant for East Berlin zoo. As we approached checkpoint Charlie, the

Part of the shipment on arrival in Soëst, before onward shipment to zoos throughout Europe. (EVB)

presence of armed soldiers was now non-existent as the wall was down by this time. A complete contrast to when I had visited East Berlin the previous time.

The unloading of the elephant was more difficult than the time before, as we were not near to an unloading bay. Consequently as soon as we dropped the tailgate, it became obvious that we would need many bales of straw to build a ramp to support underneath the tailgate so that the elephant could walk out onto a firm walkway. After some persuading, she approached the ramp and proceeded down it onto terra firma.

The elephant house itself was an impressive recent building. The Director told me that they had consulted all keepers, architects and the maintenance department for their ideas on the construction. The end product was a house that had large outside enclosures that had been designed to enable African elephants to get maximum sun. As the sun moved round to the west it would then reach the Asian elephants that in their natural environment in the jungle would not be subjected to the sun's rays because of thicker foliage and a different terrain. Inside the building, the stable areas had under floor heating and drinking water on hand at all times. This was achieved by having a small pipe, which fed a trough in the stable. This pipe was attached to a ball-cock in the service area, the idea being that when the elephant had drunk two gallons the cistern would then refill, a system that I had suggested to be implemented at Whipsnade many years ago. This was not achieved as it was deemed to be too expensive and impractical. So it was very interesting to see this set-up working successfully. Inside the building, around the circumference of the house there was a service area large enough for a small vehicle with trailer to deliver the hay and supplies. It was also used for mucking out the dens. Overall this was a most impressive house - somehow ironic in a country overshadowed by so much uncertainty.

CHAPTER 14
"In Limbo"

The weeks and months seemed to drag between cutting the cricket pitches, weeding and preparing the rugby pitch. However, after 10 months, I received a letter from Frans asking me if I would like to work for him, freelancing, on a fixed salary, transporting animals around the world. Needless to say, he had a reply from me by return of post. Excited about the prospect, I gave a month's notice at the school, having discussed my reasons with the bursar, who told me that they had been going to offer me a permanent position. He, however, understood that a job working with animals would, for me, be far preferable.

Having left the school and waiting at home for either a letter or telephone call from Frans, I decided after a week to telephone him. After great difficulty I managed to reach his secretary who told me that he had been overseas and that he would contact me within the next two days. This he did, only to tell me that the position with his Company was off, because his accountant said that it was not financially viable. So this left me unemployed for the first time in my life.

In June 1991 we moved to Harpenden into a house rented from friends. In the months that followed I did various jobs ranging from painting and decorating, gardening and putting up fencing! Then one morning I saw an advertisement in the local paper that supervisors were required at Oaklands College for either decorating or conservation skills. This was part of the Government's "Community Action" scheme. I applied and was called for an interview and successfully gained the post of "Conservation Supervisor" based at Hatfield.

My first assignment was the grounds at Astwick Manor. The participants consisted of a wide age range, male and female, from a variety of backgrounds, whose skills I would utilise in the many projects at the Manor. These consisted of repainting the aircraft hanger which housed two aircraft, which were used for training apprentices on the engines and on

John tree planting at the Wildlife Conservation Centre, St Albans. (Fr)

the aircraft in general. The other tasks included rebuilding the front of the pond, which overflowed the road, and digging out the broken overflow pipe which was a metre down so as to replace it with a new one.

The greatest task was the clearance of dead trees, shrubs and the stream that ran through the centre of the grounds, making them a haven for wildlife.

From this challenge I moved with my participants to St. Albans and Verulam Park where there is a Wildlife Conservation and Education Centre. I had an appointment with the manager of the Centre before this scheme could progress, as there was apprehension amongst their staff about my team. They were under the impression that the workers were taking part in Community Service, which was incorrect. I had to explain that they were unemployed people who had offered their skills under the Government Community Action Scheme and not offenders working off a court order! They also wanted assurance that we had the capabilities to do what was required, which included working to a given plan to redesign the Nature Garden. They also requested that the group should be limited to six, with the appropriate skills.

So work commenced here in the early spring when the materials had been purchased. These included gravel, timber, pond lining, paving, bricks, sand and cement. I had to hire machinery to level the ground, a pump to clear the pond and a cement mixer. The participants achieved the building of a pond, the laying of a circular path, the building of a brick well with a wooden canopy, a rose arch and the general landscaping of the entire garden. The Manager and his staff were so delighted with the "ground force" team that an evening party was given for the participants and the Community Action Managers.

During my time on the staff of Community Action we worked on projects for The Salvation Army, Alcoholics Anonymous, Drug Abuse Centres and Wall Hall, Aldenham, near Watford. My contract was due to terminate at the end of the year and I was given to understand that it would be renewed. As time drew nearer, I received confirmation but finally I was told that the Government had withdrawn the funding and so my employment for Community Action came to an end.

One evening whilst having dinner with our friends Margaret and Philip, it was suggested by Margaret that I might like to talk to the children on the Children's Ward at St. Albans Hospital where she worked as a teacher. So, on a number of occasions I met the children and talked to them about my work with elephants, arming myself with discarded elephant teeth and a small tusk and photographs of my work, to allow the children "hands on" experience. One particular day I spent a morning with a disturbed teenage girl who had tried unsuccessfully to take her life. She had shown a great interest, while in hospital, in animals and a desire to work with them. I felt at the end of the morning that maybe she could see a slight purpose to life which would have made my time with her worthwhile.

During this period of unemployment I gave numerous talks about elephants to many and varied organisations. I also searched world wide for work in my field - unsuccessfully, as these specialist jobs were unavailable due to unobtainable visas and permits and restriction of movements of elephants and wild animals in general. These restrictions obstructed me from returning to the work that I felt passionately about, but having said this I feel they are necessary steps for the welfare of wildlife.

It was about this time that Sheila told me about a vacancy at Homedell House, where she had been a relief Manager. This is sheltered accommodation for the elderly. Following a successful interview I started work as a relief Manager, caring for the 60 residents and the general upkeep and security of the complex. I enjoyed meeting and talking with these residents, some of whom had spent many years overseas. Occasionally, I gave talks to them about various aspects of my work and some of them told of their encounters with elephants in India where their husbands had worked.

CHAPTER 15
"And so to Japan"

Whilst working at Homedell, I again received a telephone call from my old friend Frans, who asked me if I would be interested in an assignment involving taking a young bull Asian elephant from Switzerland to Kobi in Japan. I had to explain to Frans that I would have to ask for leave for one month from my present job. Much to my delight my present employers granted this.

At the beginning of March, not feeling well due to a virus that had affected my breathing considerably, I set off for Holland. On arrival, I was met by Frans' new driver who had recently taken over from Mark. I learnt that Mark was now working in a local zoo as a keeper. My driver delivered me safely to Frans' office where I was greeted with open arms by Frans himself, his wife Elli and daughter Myraid. Over dinner and a large scotch, Frans outlined what the assignment would entail. He briefly explained how I would travel with his new driver to Rapperswil in Switzerland where I would remain for one week to become acquainted with the young bull. I would then drive with the elephant to Frankfurt Airport where we would board a jumbo jet to Osaka airport in Japan. This was the theory of Frans' plan.

Within a couple of days we set off for Switzerland, leaving Soëst in the early hours, driving through Holland into Germany, passing Cologne, Bonn, Mainz, Strasbourg and down to Zurich, eventually reaching Rapperswil Zoo, by which time we were both very tired. On our arrival we were met by the elephant trainer Mr Bremmer, who had spent all his working life in the circus. We returned to the hotel for an early night but were awakened at the crack of dawn by the hotel clerk, who informed us that Mr Bremmer was downstairs waiting to take us to work! So without any breakfast we were driven in his truck to the zoo, whereupon he informed me that training would commence with the young bull elephant every morning at 07.00 hrs to 11.00 hrs and from 14.00 hrs to 17.00 hrs for one week or until he felt confident that I had some control of the bull.

After two days contact with the young bull, who stood over six feet and weighed in the region of one tonne, Mr Bremmer decided that I should enter the circus training ring with him and as he put it "further my experience!" There were 10 full-grown cow elephants including the bull's mother and the bull himself. The elephants continued to circle around us on the command of Mr Bremmer, when he suddenly called the young bull into the centre and then handed him over to me. All went well for 10 minutes when, without any warning, he came straight at me hitting me in the chest and shoulders, propelling me straight out of the ring! It was apparent when I stood up that my shoulder had been dislocated. However, it went back, thankfully, quite easily.

A voice came from the ring "Don't just sit there, sort the animal out!" Within minutes I was back in the ring, only to be ejected once more. As I looked up at Mr Bremmer he said, "You know as well as I do that you are not an elephant keeper until you have sustained a few knocks!" This was the last time I had any real problems with "Boy."

As our early morning sessions came and went we had arrived at the point where we would have to separate this young bull from his mother Claudia. Mr Bremmer felt that Claudia would require four chains, instead of the normal two to restrain her during the crating up of the bull, which proved correct the following morning. The animal was slowly winched into the crate and then chained on front left and rear right legs. The crate was then pushed out into the yard on rollers where a crane was standing by to lift it onto the back of the lorry. Before departing, the veterinary office gave me three small phials of Valium to be injected into the animal, if necessary, during our journey to Japan.

Once at the airport, I was taken to watch the elephant crate on a large forklift truck being manoeuvred into the large cargo-hold. With the completion of the loading, the human passengers were then allowed on board. Having found my seat, I was greeted by a steward who asked me if I would check the elephant regularly during the flight. I was told of the regulation requirements when entering the cargo-hold. This involved wearing an oxygen tank on my back and obviously a facemask. The door to the hold was to the right of my seat and I made my first visit there one hour after take-off, with inquisitive looks from my fellow passengers. After my third visit to the elephant the Japanese gentleman next to me enquired if we had a problem as I seemed to be spending a lot of time "the other side of the door." I explained that we had an elephant on board and that I had to keep regular checks on him. I could tell immediately from his facial expression that he did not believe a word I had said.

After some hours into the flight the steward asked if it would be possible to sedate the elephant as the pilot said that there was movement at the rear of the aircraft. I immediately entered the hold to discover that the crate was moving on its tracks whenever the elephant moved from side to side. With my sedation kit, I climbed on top of the crate talking continuously to the young bull to reassure him of my presence. Opening the small trap door, I patted him on the rump several times before administering an injection. The animal showed no reaction to the needle. In due course the aircraft's Captain informed me that I was the only person he had ever met to have "Stuck a needle up an elephant's arse at 42,000 feet over the Urals!" This caused great hilarity amongst the rest of the crew.

Without further incident we arrived at Osaka airport in Japan at 08.30 in the morning. After the unloading of the elephant it was taken to a Customs Clearance Centre where I was to spend most of the day dealing with Japanese bureaucracy. It was 16.00 hrs before the crate could leave the Customs Area and be loaded onto the lorry for our journey to Oji Zoo, Kobe. Due to the devastation caused by the earthquake two months earlier, the normal route was out, due to broken bridges, collapsed roads and general mayhem. Consequently our route was to the harbour, where we boarded a ferry across Osaka Bay to Kobe and onto Oji Zoo.

On arrival there we were met by Masao Takita, the Vice-Director of Kobe Oji Zoo, a man of similar stature to myself and with a broad smiling face. After the usual introductions he asked me how I envisaged getting the elephant in the crate to its paddock, which was a distance from where the crane was positioned. I spoke to the crane driver who assured me that the telescopic arm would reach the elephant house. I also enquired about the strength of the cables and decided we needed six tonne as opposed to the three tonne cables that they were proposing to use. The crane driver, unable to see the elephant house once the crate was air-borne, liaised by radio with me and the Director, Mr Condor, who gave him instructions for the positioning of the crate, to be raised and then lowered into the paddock as near to the stable door as possible. Having achieved this

Kobe Oji Zoo, Japan. (DD)

remarkable feat to within four feet of the stable door, applause went up from the public and the zoo staff.

The next problem was to transfer the young bull into his stable, who by this time was not amused and probably ready to flatten me. Having inspected the stable for chain points, I found out that they were non-existent. So, I had to work out a plan that would safely transfer the elephant, a tonne of anger, into the stable. Removing the two sliding doors from the crate, one could see our friend clearly through the bars, which were now twisted and bent, making them impossible to remove. I had to arrange for them to be cut out.

The animal had been chained on the front left and rear right legs. I removed the chain from the front locking position in the crate, connected it to another chain which was then fed through into the stable and wound round the stable bars, with 10 keepers hanging on! I then slowly released the back leg chain and the elephant was gradually eased into his stable position, where he stood and relished a long drink.

An added problem was a large Asian cow elephant in the adjoining stable that was not happy with her new neighbour and was constantly trying to reach him. It was decided that two keepers would maintain a nightlong watch from the inspection area.

The next morning I decided it would be beneficial to reposition the bull out of reach of the cow. This went to plan and then the head-keeper, who appeared apprehensive, introduced me to the young bull elephant's new handler, who had previously worked with flamingos. From his facial expression I gathered he was not overjoyed at the prospect of his new responsibilities. I reassured him by telling him that we would take things very slowly through the coming weeks. The first day he spent most of his time talking and touching the animal and of course feeding and watering him. By the end of the day he felt a little more at ease! However, he would continually stand directly in front of the bull, rather than to one side, lessening the chances of his escape if the bull should suddenly lunge forward. I had my instructions translated by an interpreter who happened to be one of the zoo's vets.

The next day started, as usual, with bowing and pleasantries and coffee with the Director, who spent quite some time talking about his boyhood and his lifetime with animals. Having escaped from the office, I then reported to the elephant house for the training to commence, which this

The author outside the elephant house at Kobe Oji Zoo, Japan. (DD)

day consisted of bathing and cleaning the animal down, foot procedures and the removal of ankle chains to the diagonally opposite leg. On a good day one would hope to get six hours of training completed. This was not always the case as the trainees were often removed to other departments, and rest times had to be observed. After a few days I insisted that my trainees remained with me for the entire day, as otherwise the continuity we were building up with the bull would suffer.

One morning at breakfast in the hotel the daughter of the Proprietor greeted me, with a large grin on her face and holding a newspaper in her hand. Unfolding it, she exposed a picture of myself and the bull elephant taken at Oji Zoo the previous day. "This is you," she said, and consequently I was able to order anything, within reason, for breakfast including toast, omelette and hard-boiled eggs!! That's what fame does for you!

Progress at the zoo was slow due to the boisterous behaviour of the bull and the uncertainty of the keepers, but as the weeks went past I took a less prominent part in the handling of the bull and I could see that gradually their confidence was growing. I could not emphasise the safety aspect of handling bull elephants enough, as their animal would, one day, be a full-grown bull and they would be subjected to the phenomenon of musth, a natural state that a male elephant goes through annually, after he has attained the age of maturity.

The Director told me he was very satisfied and content with the way in which the training was progressing. He then went on to say that I should stay longer to see the cherry trees in blossom, but with my deteriorating breathing I felt that I should leave on the planned departure date as the demolition of buildings, due to recent earthquakes, was continuous and the dust was everywhere.

Naturally enough, I often reflect on my work with animals and newspaper articles constantly remind me that elephants need to be treated with caution. In my view training and rapport are crucial in the safe keeping of elephants in captivity. These are large mammals and you need to be constantly vigilant for the dangers that are always there, particularly if they are mistreated, frightened or overexcited.

In recent years I was to read about my favourite elephant, Kumara, who you will recall was moved to Chester Zoo in 1989. Kumara had been at Whipsnade for close on 25 years, and when the move was proposed I always felt a major change such as this would create extra stress and pose

The grounds at Kobe Oji Zoo, Japan. (DD)

179

The author with Mr M. Condor, Director of Kobe Oji Zoo, Japan. (DD)

The author with Director and staff at Kobe Oji Zoo, Japan. (DD)

hidden dangers for the new staff. Like humans, elephants don't readily accept change. Sadly there was an incident at Chester when a keeper working with Kumara was fatally injured. Some time later Kumara was put down, reportedly due to ill health - a sad day for all who had known and worked with her, me included.

As late as 2002, the dangers involved in keeping elephants were highlighted yet again in the national press when it was announced that London Zoo would no longer be displaying elephants - a major change since they had been an attraction right from 1831 when elephants were first kept at the zoo.

Once again a fatal accident involving the senior keeper, Jim Robson, may have precipitated the transfer of three female elephants to Whipsnade Wild Animal Park to join the existing herd, which now numbers 7 - six females and one bull called Emmett. Incidentally, this move will bring together again Anna, Kaylee, Lucha and Mya, four of the elephants I selected and brought back from Burma more than ten years ago.

With this larger herd I personally hope that the zoo will continue to promote "hands on" or "free contact" management of the elephants - in other words contact and training between man and beast. If you keep elephants in zoos it is vital that they not only have the right facilities, space and care, but also the personal training that is so vital to their health and wellbeing. I do not believe that the adoption of "protected" or "limited" contact is the correct humane approach for elephants in captivity.

Looking back over the past 40 years of involvement with animals, they have given me tremendous enjoyment, a sense of achievement and great satisfaction. Such work has been my lifetime hobby, and the feeling of no "Monday morning blues" cannot be the experience of many employees. The daily greeting I received from my elephants is something that will be with me forever. The elephant house would echo with trumpets and roars so dramatically that Owen Chamberlain, the Park Manager, would frequently comment to his wife as they drank their tea in the kitchen some 500 yards from the elephant compound "John's in early again!"

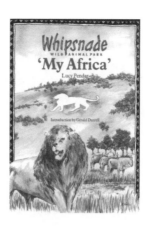

WHIPSNADE MY AFRICA
by Lucy Pendar

The inside story of sixty years of this world-renowned institution, written from the unique viewpoint of a young girl living and growing up in Sir Peter Chalmers Mitchell's dream of an open-plan Zoo Park, the first of its kind in this country. Her father was the Resident Engineer who took her to Whipsnade Park just before it opened, thus leading her into an enchanted childhood.

As well as tracing the Park's full history, the book is full of anecdotes, both humorous and tragic, about its animals and people - all of whom she has known down the years. Despite eventually moving away in adult life, her enduring love affair with the place has never faltered. She has felt compelled to return again and again to follow its changing fortunes. With over 130 fascinating rare photographs and original line drawings, the book also contains an introduction by Gerald Durrell.

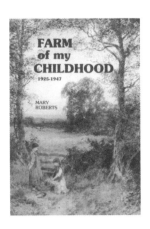

FARM OF MY CHILDHOOD
by Mary Roberts

A way of life in the countryside that has almost disappeared - a young girl on a remote farm near Flitwick in Bedfordshire some fifty years ago. A free and happy childhood centred on a rambling old farmhouse - much of her time spent with the farm workers and the animals she loved so much. Riding her pony along the lanes and byways, walking along the footpaths past thatched cottages, enjoying the woodlands and gathering the wild flowers, or paddling in the clear sparkling brooks and streams.

Sometimes in her wanderings she would pass the artist Sylvester Stannard happily preserving such scenes for posterity in his well-loved watercolours, as Mary Roberts now does in her truly evocative word-pictures.

A LASTING IMPRESSION
by Michael Dundrow

Michael Dundrow experienced an event in his formative years which strongly coloured or even completely changed the rest of his life.

This book describes one boy's overwhelming experience - wartime evacuation - which has left a truly lasting impression on his adult life. For this twelve year old from London's East End, to be dumped among a family of strangers on a large and busy farm below the Chilterns in Bedfordshire was a make or break experience of the first order.

Enriched by his years on the farm and in the village of Totternhoe, the adventures of his new found friends, the sheer interest, fun and hard work of farm life and also the sowing of the seeds of appreciation of that lovely corner of South Bedfordshire, the details are all here, written with great affection. Although written fifty years after these unforgettable things happened, the story is undimmed by the passage of time.

In this evocative picture of wartime England are many glimpses of a way of village and farm life that has altered so dramatically in recent years as to be almost unrecognisable today.

Books Published by THE BOOK CASTLE

COUNTRYSIDE CYCLING IN BEDFORDSHIRE, BUCKINGHAMSHIRE AND HERTFORDSHIRE: Mick Payne. Twenty rides on and off-road for all the family.

PUB WALKS FROM COUNTRY STATIONS: Bedfordshire and Hertfordshire: Clive Higgs. Fourteen circular country rambles, each starting and finishing at a railway station and incorporating a pub stop at a mid way point.

PUB WALKS FROM COUNTRY STATIONS: Buckinghamshire and Oxfordshire: Clive Higgs. Circular rambles incorporating pub-stops.

LOCAL WALKS: South Bedfordshire and North Chilterns: Vaughan Basham. Twenty-seven thematic circular walks.

LOCAL WALKS: North and Mid Bedfordshire: Vaughan Basham. Twenty-five thematic circular walks.

FAMILY WALKS: Chilterns South: Nick Moon. Thirty 3 to 5 mile circular walks.

FAMILY WALKS: Chilterns North: Nick Moon. Thirty shorter circular walks.

CHILTERN WALKS: Hertfordshire, Bedfordshire and North Bucks: Nick Moon.

CHILTERN WALKS: Buckinghamshire: Nick Moon.

CHILTERN WALKS: Oxfordshire and West Buckinghamshire: Nick Moon. A trilogy of circular walks, in association with the Chiltern Society. Each volume contains 30 circular walks.

OXFORDSHIRE WALKS: Oxford, the Cotswolds and the Cherwell Valley: Nick Moon.

OXFORDSHIRE WALKS: Oxford, the Downs and the Thames Valley: Nick Moon. Two volumes that complement Chiltern Walks: Oxfordshire, and complete coverage of the county, in association with the Oxford Fieldpaths Society. Thirty circular walks in each.

THE D'ARCY DALTON WAY: Nick Moon. Long-distance footpath across the Oxfordshire Cotswolds and Thames Valley, with various circular walk suggestions.

THE CHILTERN WAY: Nick Moon. A guide to the new 133 mile circular Long-Distance Path through Bedfordshire, Buckinghamshire, Hertfordshire and Oxfordshire, as planned by the Chiltern Society.

CHANGES IN OUR LANDSCAPE: Aspects of Bedfordshire, Buckinghamshire and the Chilterns 1947-1992: Eric Meadows. Over 350 photographs from the author's collection spanning nearly 50 years.

JOURNEYS INTO BEDFORDSHIRE: Anthony Mackay. Foreword by The Marquess of Tavistock, Woburn Abbey. A lavish book of over 150 evocative ink drawings.

COCKNEY KID & COUNTRYMEN: Ted Enever. The Second World War remembered by the children of Woburn Sands and Aspley Guise. A six year old boy is evacuated from London's East End to start life in a Buckinghamshire village.

CHANGING FACES, CHANGING PLACES: Post war Bletchley and Woburn Sands 1945-1970 Ted Enever. Evocative memoirs of post-war life on the Beds/Bucks borders, up to the coming of Milton Keynes new town.

BUCKINGHAM AT WAR: Pip Brimson. Stories of courage, humour and pathos as Buckingham people adapt to war.

WINGS OVER WING: The Story of a World War II Bomber Training Unit: Mike Warth. The activities of RAF Wing in Buckinghamshire.

JOURNEYS INTO BUCKINGHAMSHIRE: Anthony Mackay. Superb line drawings plus background text: large format landscape gift book.

BUCKINGHAMSHIRE MURDERS: Len Woodley. Nearly two centuries of nasty crimes.

WINGRAVE: A Rothschild Village in the Vale: Margaret and Ken Morley. Thoroughly researched and copiously illustrated survey of the last 200 years in this lovely village between Aylesbury and Leighton Buzzard.

HISTORIC FIGURES IN THE BUCKINGHAMSHIRE LANDSCAPE: John Houghton. Major personalities and events that have shaped the county's past, including Bletchley Park.

TWICE UPON A TIME: John Houghton. North Bucks short stories loosely based on fact.

SANCTITY AND SCANDAL IN BEDS AND BUCKS: John Houghton. A miscellany of unholy people and events.

MANORS and MAYHEM, PAUPERS and PARSONS: Tales from Four Shires: Beds., Bucks., Herts. and Northants: John Houghton. Little known historical snippets and stories.

THE LAST PATROL: Policemen killed on duty while serving the Thames Valley: Len Woodley.

FOLK: Characters and Events in the History of Bedfordshire and Northamptonshire: Vivienne Evans. Anthology of people of yesteryear -arranged alphabetically by village or town.

JOHN BUNYAN: His Life and Times: Vivienne Evans. Highly praised and readable account.

THE RAILWAY AGE IN BEDFORDSHIRE: Fred Cockman. Classic, illustrated account of early railway history.

A LASTING IMPRESSION: Michael Dundrow. A boyhood evacuee recalls his years in the Chiltern village of Totternhoe near Dunstable.

ELEPHANTS I'LL NEVER FORGET: A Keeper's Life at Whipsnade and London Zoo: John Weatherhead. Experiences, dramatic and sad, from a lifetime with these well-loved giants.

WHIPSNADE MY AFRICA: Lucy Pendar. The inside story of sixty years of this world-renowned institution. Full of history, anecdotes, stories of animals and people.

GLEANINGS REVISITED: Nostalgic Thoughts of a Bedfordshire Farmer's Boy: E.W. O'Dell. His own sketches and early photographs adorn this lively account of rural Bedfordshire in days gone by.

BEDFORDSHIRE'S YESTERYEARS: The Rural Scene: Brenda Fraser-Newstead. Vivid first-hand accounts of country life two or three generations ago.

BEDFORDSHIRE'S YESTERYEARS: Craftsmen and Tradespeople: Brenda Fraser-Newstead. Fascinating recollections over several generations practising many vanishing crafts and trades.

BEDFORDSHIRE'S YESTERYEARS: War Times and Civil Matters: Brenda Fraser-Newstead. Two World Wars, plus transport, law and order, etc.

DUNNO'S ORIGINALS: A facsimile of the rare pre-Victorian history of Dunstable and surrounding villages. New preface and glossary by John Buckledee, Editor of The Dunstable Gazette.

DUNSTABLE DOWN THE AGES: Joan Schneider and Vivienne Evans. Succinct overview of the town's prehistory and history - suitable for all ages.

HISTORIC INNS OF DUNSTABLE: Vivienne Evans. Illustrated booklet, especially featuring ten pubs in the town centre.

EXPLORING HISTORY ALL AROUND: Vivienne Evans. Planned as seven circular car tours, plus background to places of interest en-route in Bedfordshire and parts of Bucks and Herts.

PROUD HERITAGE: A Brief History of Dunstable, 1000-2000AD: Vivienne Evans. Century by century account of the town's rich tradition and key events, many of national significance.

DUNSTABLE WITH THE PRIORY: 1100-1550: Vivienne Evans. Dramatic growth of Henry I's important new town around a major crossroads.

DUNSTABLE IN TRANSITION: 1550-1700: Vivienne Evans. Wealth of original material as the town evolves without the Priory.

DUNSTABLE DECADE: THE EIGHTIES: A Collection of Photographs: Pat Lovering. A souvenir book of nearly 300 pictures of people and events in the 1980's

STREETS AHEAD: An Illustrated Guide to the Origins of Dunstable's Street Names: Richard Walden. Fascinating text and captions to hundreds of photographs, past and present, throughout the town.

DUNSTABLE IN DETAIL: Nigel Benson. A hundred of the town's buildings and features, plus town trail map.

DUNSTAPLE: A Tale of The Watling Highway: A.W. Mooring. Dramatic novelisation of Dunstable's legend of Dunne the Robber - reprinted after a century out of print.

25 YEARS OF DUNSTABLE: Bruce Turvey. Reissue of this photographic treasure-trove of the town up to the Queen's Silver Jubilee, 1952-77.

DUNSTABLE SCHOOL: 1888-1971. F.M. Bancroft. Short history of one of the town's most influential institutions.

BOURNE and BRED: A Dunstable Boyhood Between the Wars: Colin Bourne. An elegantly written, well illustrated book capturing the spirit of the town over fifty years ago.

OLD HOUGHTON: Pat Lovering. Pictorial record capturing the changing appearances of Houghton Regis over the past 100 years.

ROYAL HOUGHTON: Pat Lovering. Illustrated history of Houghton Regis from the earliest of times to the present.

WERE YOU BEING SERVED?: Remembering 50 Luton Shops of Yesteryear: Bob Norman. Well-illustrated review of the much loved, specialist outlets of a generation or two ago.

GIRLS IN BLUE: Christine Turner. The activities of the famous Luton Girls Choir properly documented over its 41 year period from 1936 to 1977.

THE STOPSLEY BOOK: James Dyer. Definitive, detailed account of this historic area of Luton. 150 rare photographs.

THE STOPSLEY PICTURE BOOK: James Dyer. New material and photographs make an ideal companion to The Stopsley Book.

PUBS and PINTS: The Story of Luton's Public Houses and Breweries: Stuart Smith. The background to beer in the town, plus hundreds of photographs, old and new.

LUTON AT WAR - VOLUME ONE: As compiled by the Luton News in 1947, a well illustrated thematic account.

LUTON AT WAR - VOLUME TWO: Second part of the book compiled by The Luton News.

THE CHANGING FACE OF LUTON: An Illustrated History: Stephen Bunker, Robin Holgate and Marian Nichols. Luton's development from earliest times to the present busy industrial town. Illustrated in colour and mono.

WHERE THEY BURNT THE TOWN HALL DOWN: Luton, The First World War and the Peace Day Riots, July 1919: Dave Craddock. Detailed analysis of a notorious incident.

THE MEN WHO WORE STRAW HELMETS: Policing Luton, 1840-1974: Tom Madigan. Fine chronicled history, many rare photographs; author~served in Luton Police for fifty years.

BETWEEN THE HILLS: The Story of Lilley, a Chiltern Village: Roy Pinnock. A priceless piece of our heritage - the rural beauty remains but the customs and way of life described here have largely disappeared.

KENILWORTH SUNSET: A Luton Town Supporter's Journal: Tim Kingston. Frank and funny account of football's ups and downs.

A HATTER GOES MAD!: Kristina Howells. Luton Town footballers, officials and supporters talk to a female fan.

LEGACIES: Tales and Legends of Luton and the North Chilterns: Vic Lea. Mysteries and stories based on fact, including Luton Town Football Club. Many photographs.

THREADS OF TIME: Shela Porter. The life of a remarkable mother and businesswoman, spanning the entire century and based in Hitchin and (mainly) Bedford.

FARM OF MY CHILDHOOD, 1925-1947: Mary Roberts. An almost vanished lifestyle on a remote farm near Flitwick.

STICKS AND STONES: The Life and Times of a Journeyman Printer in Hertford, Dunstable, Cheltenham and Wolverton: Harry Edwards.

CRIME IN HERTFORDSHIRE Volume 1 Law and Disorder: Simon Walker. Authoritative, detailed survey of the changing legal process over many centuries.

JOURNEYS INTO HERTFORDSHIRE: Anthony Mackay. A foreword by The Marquis of Salisbury, Hatfield House. Introducing nearly 200 superbly detailed line drawings.

LEAFING THROUGH LITERATURE: Writers' Lives in Herts and Beds: David Carroll. Illustrated short biographies of many famous authors and their connections with these counties.

A PILGRIMAGE IN HERTFORDSHIRE: H.M. Alderman. Classic, between-the-wars tour round the county, embellished with line drawings.

THE VALE OF THE NIGHTINGALE: Molly Andrews. Several generations of a family, lived against a Harpenden backdrop.

SUGAR MICE AND STICKLEBACKS: Childhood Memories of a Hertfordshire Lad: HarryEdwards.Vivid evocation of gentle pre-war in an archetypal village, Hertingfordbury.

SWANS IN MY KITCHEN: Lis Dorer. Story of a Swan Sanctuary near Hemel Hempstead.

MYSTERIOUS RUINS: The Story of Sopwell, St.Albans: Donald Pelletier. Still one of the town's most atmospheric sites. Sopwell's history is full of fluctuations and interest, mainly as a nunnery associated with St.Albans Abbey.

THE HILL OF THE MARTYR: An Architectural History of St.Albans Abbey: Eileen Roberts. Scholarly and readable chronological narrative history of Hertfordshire and Bedfordshire's famous cathedral. Fully illustrated with photographs and plans.

THE TALL HITCHIN INSPECTOR'S CASEBOOK: A Victorian Crime Novel Based on Fact: Edgar Newman. Worthies of the time encounter more archetypal villains.

SPECIALLY FOR CHILDREN

VILLA BELOW THE KNOLLS: A Story of Roman Britain: Michael Dundrow. An exciting adventure for young John in Totternhoe and Dunstable two thousand years ago.

THE RAVENS: One Boy Against the Might of Rome: James Dyer. On the Barton Hills and in the south-east of England as the men of the great fort of Ravensburgh (near Hexton) confront the invaders.

TITLES ACQUIRED BY THE BOOK CASTLE

BEDFORDSHIRE WILDLIFE: B.S. Nau, C.R. Boon, J.P. Knowles for the Bedfordshire Natural History Society. Over 200 illustrations, maps, photographs and tables survey the plants and animals of this varied habitat.

BIRDS OF BEDFORDSHIRE: Paul Trodd and David Kramer. Environments, breeding maps and details of 267 species, with dozens of photographs, illustrations and diagrams.

A BEDFORDSHIRE QUIZ BOOK: Eric G. Meadows. Wide ranging quizzes and picture puzzles on the history, people, places and bygones of the county.

CURIOSITIES OF BEDFORDSHIRE: A County Guide to the Unusual: Pieter and Rita Boogaart.
Quirky, well-illustrated survey of little-known features throughout the county.

THE BIRDS OF HERTFORDSHIRE: Tom Gladwin and Bryan Sage. Essays, maps and records for all 297 species, plus illustrations, photographs and other plates.

BUTTERFLIES OF HERTFORDSHIRE: Brian Sawford. History and ecological guide, with colour photographs and maps for nearly 50 species.

WELWYN RAILWAYS: Tom Gladwin, Peter Neville, Douglas White. A history of the Great Northern line from 1850 to 1986, as epitomised by the five mile stretch between Welwyn Garden City and Woolmer Green. Profusely illustrated in colour and black and white - landscape format.

LIFE AND TIMES OF THE GREAT EASTERN RAILWAY (1839-1922): Harry Paar and Adrian Gray. Personalities, accidents, traffic and tales, plus contemporary photographs and old o.s. maps of this charming railway that transformed East Anglia and Hertfordshire between 1839 and 1922.

THE QUACK: Edgar Newman. Imaginative faction featuring characters in a nineteenth-century painting of a busy Hitchin market scene - especially quack doctor William Mansell.

D-DAY TO ARNHEIM - with Hertfordshire's Gunners: Major Robert Kiln. Vivid, personal accounts of the D-Day preparations and drama, and the subsequent Normandy battles, plus photographs and detailed campaign maps.

THE BOOK CASTLE
12 Church Street, Dunstable
Bedfordshire LU5 4RU
Tel: (01582) 605670 Fax (01582) 662431
Email: bc@book-castle.co.uk
Website: www.book-castle.co.uk